A REMEDY for Itching Ears

CHRISTIAN DOCTRINE REMIXED FOR A NEW GENERATION OF BELIEVERS.

DR. JESSE T. WILLIAMS, JR.

Copyright © 2011 by Dr. Jesse T. Williams, Jr.

All rights reserved. No part of this book may be used, reproduced, stored in a retrieval system, or transmitted in any form whatsoever — including electronic, photocopy, recording — without prior written permission from the author, except in the case of brief quotations embodied in critical articles or reviews.

All scripture quotations, unless otherwise indicated, are taken from the *Holy Bible, King James Version. KJV.* Public Domain.

FIRST EDITION, SECOND PRINTING

ISBN: 978-1-936989-59-1

Published by
NewBookPublishing.com, a division of Reliance Media, Inc.
2395 Apopka Blvd., #200, Apopka, FL 32703
NewBookPublishing.com

Printed in the United States of America

Dedication

This book is dedicated to my immediate and extended family who are a never-ending source of encouragement and inspiration to me daily; to the many peers in this Gospel ministry with whom God has blessed me to enjoy countless hours of friendship, fellowship and counsel; and to the Convent Avenue Baptist Church family of Harlem, New York, for being a faithful church of excellence that loves and prays for its pastor and strives daily to be *Changed People, Changing the Community and the World for Jesus Christ.*

Foreword

"For the time will come when they will not endure sound doctrine; but after their own lusts shall they heap to themselves teachers, having itching ears; And they shall turn away their ears from the truth, and shall be turned unto fables. But watch thou in all things...make full proof of thy ministry."
(II Timothy 4:3-5)

These words of the Apostle Paul to Timothy in 66 or 67 A.D. are words not trapped in the antiquity of the ancient New Testament world. These words are as contemporary as our latest breath. We are, indeed, living in a Post Modern age in which there are no absolutes. In the words of a Broadway play "Everything nailed down is coming loose." I am of the firm belief that the church has weakened over the years primarily because we no longer preach and teach with regularity the great doctrines of the Christian faith. Without careful and prayerful understanding of Christian doctrines we lose what is foundational in our comprehension of Jesus Christ and what must be embraced by His Church. It is no wonder that many who claim faith in Christ are not able to defend and witness to their faith because of a woeful ignorance as to what they do not know.

How refreshing that a voice arises during this season when doctrinal preaching and teaching appear to be on sabbatical. Dr. Jesse T. Williams has painstakingly placed before us this much- needed work that calls us back to the Christian fundamentals of our faith. Simplistic, yet profound, is this Pastor- Preacher-Scholar's approach to those things "most surely believed among us" (St. Luke 1:1). Many within our ecclesiastical ranks must bow in shame when asked the question, "When last did you hear, preached or taught, such doctrines of the faith as the atonement; sanctification; justification; salvation; regeneration – just to name a few?"

I salute Dr. Williams for his bold initiative in this regard, for like Luke, he has purposed to place before us a clear and concise presentation of the doctrines of the Christian faith. Mind you – this work is more than a theological reflection. This work represents that which has been taught in the context of the historic Convent Avenue Baptist Church of Harlem. Thus, this is a manual whose intention is to broaden the thinking of the local church and saturate her congregants with an understanding of those doctrinal tenets so crucial for Christian growth and development.

May you read and digest these leaves and in doing so feel the fresh breath of the Holy Spirit. Your discipleship will be greatly deepened because of this read.

Dr. Charles E. Booth, *Pastor*
Mt. Olivet Baptist Church
Columbus, Ohio

When I reflect upon the state of the church in America I am both happy and saddened by what I see. There are wonderfully gifted men and women who are faithfully teaching and preaching the word of God, but, at the same time, there are others who have failed to grasp the great and awesome responsibility to "rightly divide the word of truth." I do not believe that it is, in every case, a matter of people not caring about the truth and its faithful application, but, rather, it is a matter of people not having been taught the truth in a manner that was easy for them to grasp. It appears that there are people from the pulpit to the back pew who are uninformed and ill equipped to discern or discuss the faith once delivered to the saints.

Enter Pastor Jesse T. Williams, who is both scholar and practitioner. He has undertaken the task of helping the church to equip the saints for the work of the ministry by putting in layman's terms the articles of faith of the Church. This is an important work for the African American Church in that much of the material that is used by African American churches has been written and produced by people who do not share our particular history, insights or struggles. Hence, some of the opinions and interpretive tools used to teach this material do not speak to contemporary African American culture. His work on the eighteen articles of faith of the church is thorough, yet easy to read; but as an added bonus, Dr. Williams peaks over the balcony of hope and history and deals with some topics that traditionally have not been a part of the Articles of Faith, but probably should have been. He has taken the time to work out some new Articles of Faith that respond to the realities and needs of the 21st century. This work is a welcomed addition to the other works that have preceded it and will be a helpful tool in helping the church to understand who we are to be and what we are to believe. As his pastor and his friend of 25 years, I commend him and recommend his work to you without reservation. It will be a blessing to the body of Christ and to the people called Baptists, in particular.

    Ronald L. Bobo, Sr., D. Min. *Senior Pastor*
    West Side Missionary Baptist Church
    St. Louis, Missouri

Doctrine. This is a strange and even scary word among many church attendees who fill the pews across the width and breadth of this land, particularly within the context of the Black Baptist Church. The unfortunate experience is many Christians do not know what we believe and this is rather pronounced within the Black Baptist Church. In scanning the Biblical writ, Paul states in II Timothy 4:3-4 *"For the time is coming when people will not put up with sound doctrine, but having itching ears, they will accumulate for themselves teachers to suit their own desires, and will turn away from listening to the truth and wander away to myths"* (NRSV).

This is the reality within the local church that makes us impotent and ignorant when it comes to appreciating, understanding, and even defending the faith. I believe most African American Baptist Churches have approximately 90% of the congregation who are unaware of what it means to be Baptist and Christian. In fact, I have discovered in my new member's class that most people join the Baptist church because of family ties or social status rather than an intentional expressive way to live out faith. Unfortunately, most African American Baptist churches (rural, urban, and suburban) lack doctrinal focus to instill in its congregants basic tenets of the faith, particularly from a Baptist perspective. And I believe part of the problem may be the lack of interest coupled with tedious boredom that surrounds the study of Baptist doctrine.

However, we have in this presentation of Baptist doctrines and beliefs, as Dr. Charles Booth, Senior Pastor of Mt. Olivet Baptist Church (Columbus, OH) and nationally known revivalist, would say, "a bucket being dipped in an old well to bring up fresh water." In this rendering, Dr. Jesse T. Williams has given the African American Baptist church a major and prolific resource to empower the local church body with insights, wisdom, and practical every day application of who we are, why we exist, what we should be doing, and how we should be living in this age of apostasy and heretical teachings that have infiltrated quite a few local Baptist congregations.

By giving us the "Remix", Dr. Williams aptly suggests and supports that our doctrinal beliefs give us the capacity to deal with social justice issues while, simultaneously pursuing the evangelical thrust of the Great Commission that Jesus provides in Matthew 28:18-20. In everyday language, this book provides exposition, elucidation, and emphasis on the eighteen Articles of Faith that most Baptist churches subscribe. Nevertheless, it transcends the narrowness of denomination because most Protestant congregations have some semblance of this doctrinal construct. The readability of this powerful presentation will make it a MUST for new member classes. It has ignited a passion for me to share with my local context the need to understand and appreciate, "Why we believe what we believe." It will bless you as it has me and hopefully, help African American Baptist churches re-establish themselves on a strong foundation while maintaining autonomy from a governance perspective and soothe those itching ears.

Reverend Dr. Robert Charles Scott, *Senior Pastor*
Central Baptist Church
Saint Louis, Missouri

Table of Contents

Dedication 3

Forewords 5

Introduction 13

PART I.

What Do We Believe? 21

Chapter 1

The Scriptures and our True God 41

Chapter 2

The Fall of Man, Salvation, and Justification 57

Chapter 3

Understanding the Freeness of
Salvation and Regeneration 73

Chapter 4

Moving on to Repentance and Faith,
God's Purpose of Grace, and True Sanctification 85

Chapter 5

The Saints, the Law, the Gospel, and a Gospel Church 101

Chapter 6

Baptism, the Lord's Supper, and the Christian Sabbath 119

Table of Contents *Continued*

Chapter 7

How Does Civil Government Fit With it All? 133

Chapter 8

The Righteous, the Wicked, and the World to Come........... 141

PART II.

What Else Do We Believe?.. 151

Chapter 9

How We Really Live Beyond the Articles of Faith 153

Chapter 10

Worship, Prayer and Discipleship.. 159

Chapter 11

Missions, Evangelism, and Stewardship 175

Chapter 12

Applying our Spiritual Gifts and
Understanding Social Justice Ministry 189

About the Author 203

Order Information 205

Introduction

We can't take it for granted anymore…

A recent article that appeared in the New York Times entitled, *Basic Religion Test Stumps Many Americans*, (The New York Times, 28 September 2010, Laurie Goodstein) pointed out a sad but true reality that both clergy and laity have known about today's church for quite some time; Christians in general don't really know much about their religion or how to articulate it in meaningful ways. The article is based on research conducted by an independent firm that phoned more than 3,400 Americans and asked them 32 questions about the Bible, Christianity and other world religions. The results were quite startling. Those who scored highest were atheists and agnostics! On average, people who took the survey answered half of the questions incorrectly, and many even answered questions about their own personal faith tradition incorrectly.

The results of this study point out the reality that the average Christian of today has an inadequate understanding of the basic tenets of his or her faith. It seems to be a cultural norm now in this era of

Post-modernity that the basic doctrinal teachings of the church have become devalued in favor of a more personalized approach to religious belief. In other words, one of the casualties of Post-modernity is that people have embraced a paradigm of believing whatever they want to without regard to the historical or theological foundational teachings of Christian churches and denominations. How did we get here? When did this happen? It hasn't always been this way in American church culture.

It used to be, before the dawning of post-modernity, that there were a lot of people in our neighborhoods, cities and churches that were what we referred to as *"raised in the church"*. By this, we often meant that this person was not only someone who had attended church regularly and consistently from birth; but that his or her parents, family, friends and extended family were also actively connected and grounded in the life of the church. In fact, the church was the institution that was at the center of our lives; spiritually, socially, economically, educationally, and in most every other way. Church membership and church life were critically important to who we were. It was understood that being connected to a church was how we lived and what we did in order to properly order our lives and fit into society. It wasn't an option whether or not children attended church because parents brought their children to church regularly and consistently. It was not unusual for children to find themselves accompanying their parents to church three times on Sunday for worship and Christian Education; and another four to five times throughout the week for various meetings and activities that occurred at the church. Our parents held offices and positions of responsibility in the church, and we grew up watching them do church work and hearing them talk church talk.

As a result of the experience of being immersed in church life so deeply and consistently, we learned about the church and church people through the process of enculturation. We learned the language, the rituals, the practices and the norms of the church because we saw and heard them lived out and articulated on a daily basis in the church, the home, the neighborhood, and even in the school. We learned what appropriate behavior should be in the church; and who could and should do what in the church.

Not surprisingly then, we also learned about what our doctrinal beliefs were. Through sermons, Sunday school class, bible study, hymns, and the teaching of our parents, we learned what we believe and how to talk about it. We all became *"armchair theologians"* of a sort because we were so immersed in church life for so long that it became our lens or paradigm through which we viewed all of life. So, we reflected on what we believed and talked about how it applied to our daily living. And, we critiqued our experience of what it meant to be *"raised in the church"* versus what it meant to be in a relationship with God through Jesus Christ.

While being raised in the church was surely a blessing to many of us who had that experience, in this post-modern age as God draws new people to the church, it's something that we can no longer take for granted. The reality in our culture today is that there are many people who were *not* raised in the church. Their childhood and upbringing may not have included any involvement in church or religion at all. As I speak with Pastors across the length and breadth of this country, it has become blatantly obvious to me that God is drawing people to the church in this present age who may have never been in the church before. Church life and organized religion is foreign to them, their family and their friends. Their parents did not actively bring them to church with any consistency or regularity, so therefore, the church is not the center of their lives and community the way it was for those raised in the church. They've not been actively involved in church work, they've not been exposed to church talk, and they've not been immersed in the rituals and norms of church life like many have been. It is not surprising then, that some people may come into the church having no theological framework for organizing and understanding what they believe and why they believe it. So, they have no clear method to articulate their faith so it can be shared with others in a mutually beneficial way.

And yet, God lovingly calls all of us into the body of Christ to be believers and disciples who love and care for each other and who stand as living witnesses to the reality of God's love and activity in the world. So, whether we were raised in the church or not, God calls all of us, and God has purpose for all of us. In order for individuals and churches to be effective witnesses for Jesus Christ in this world, we have to know what we believe and be able to articulate it and proclaim it in meaningful ways. Particularly in this post-modern age, which is characterized by so much religious pluralism, it is important that Christians know what they believe and be able to confess it openly and unashamedly as witnesses in the world. If we don't know what we believe, then we can easily be *tossed back and forth by the winds of strange doctrine;* especially in this culture in which we now live.

Whether we were raised in the church or not, God calls all of us, and God has purpose for all of us.

One of the startling revelations in the church regarding doctrinal understanding is that there are still even some who *were raised in the church* who don't know what they believe or how to articulate it. It is not only those who came into the church from the outside who need doctrinal clarity; there are also many who were raised in the church for whom the processes of enculturation and osmosis did not work, or at least they did not completely connect people with a well-grounded theological framework from which to talk about what they believe and why. So, we can't take it for granted that those raised in the church understand their faith to the point where they can talk about it either.

The purpose of this book is not to suggest that all of us in the church can or should be doctrinal experts. The very nature of theology and doctrine is that of a journey, not a destination. We never reach a point where we have mastered the entire body of knowledge about God and the church: That's not humanly possible, even for trained clergy. The journey toward greater understanding of what we believe is best done in the context of a congregation being guided and taught by a Pastor. It involves meaningful dialogue, questions, discussions and reflection upon both individual and congregational experiences with God and the bible. The most valuable learning happens while we are traveling on the journey and remaining faithful to God, so it is my desire that this book would serve as a starting point for teaching and creating dialogue within the local church so that both laity and clergy alike will have a frame- work for knowing what they believe, why they believe it, and have the ability to articulate it in some basic format.

In general, I have attempted to deal with two primary questions in this book. **First**, what do people, who are totally new to the church and church life, need to know and be able to articulate about the basic doctrinal teachings of their faith in order to fulfill the purpose that God has for their lives? **Secondly**, what do those who are already established in the church who either never learned or have forgotten some of the basic doctrinal teachings of their faith need to know in order to more fully participate in the church and fulfill the purpose that God has for their lives in the church and the kingdom of God?

In light of that, this book is not intended to be one that delves into some new unchartered depths of technical, historical, doctrinal analysis, nor is it intended to engage in gregarious theological gymnastics that are meant to impress clergy, scholars or theologians in the academy. This book is written to be "user-friendly" and practical. Hence, these pages represent the reflections and teachings shared by a church pastor who loves God, the church and its' people; and who is concerned with empowering and equipping lay people in the church with a foundation and framework from which they can talk about their faith and articulate what they believe and why in this Post-modern age.

If these reflections and teachings can help other Pastors and congregations who are on the same journey and are struggling with the same questions and challenges, then to God be the glory! This work is not being presented as a definitive authority or reference when it comes to doctrinal belief, rather, it is a guidepost that will hopefully help pastors and congregations begin a wonderful journey of learning and sharing together.

If anything, this book is designed to help clergy and laity ask different kinds of questions regarding doctrinal beliefs for the purpose of learning them with greater clarity. I am convinced that all theology and doctrinal study is done best when we ask the new questions and reason together with God, the Bible and one another in the church to arrive at answers that will enlighten and enhance our understanding of God, the church, our faith and one another. Let the journey begin!

PART I.

What Do We Believe?

Introduction To The Articles Of Faith

For as long as I can remember, the document known as "The Articles of Faith" has been the definitive treasure chest of doctrinal teaching in my faith tradition. I was raised and nurtured in the Baptist faith, which is characterized by autonomous local congregations that affiliate with larger denominational bodies voluntarily. As far back as I can remember in my church life, whenever something significant of a doctrinal nature was to be discussed, taught or celebrated, the Articles of Faith along with the Bible were the authoritative standards by which any and all teaching and understanding were judged. Whenever a minister was to be ordained for the purpose of going into full-time ministry or the pastorate, he or she was told to study and thoroughly familiarize themselves with the Articles of Faith. In some cases, candidates for ordination were even encouraged to memorize the Articles and be proficient in reciting them in order to pass the examination. Laity in the church, however, were rarely encouraged to get an in-depth understanding of the Articles of Faith.

The 18 Articles of Faith, as they currently appear, form a

framework and foundation of some of the basic doctrinal teachings that Baptists adhere to. When one delves into the history and formation of the Articles, he or she soon discovers that the Articles were revised and formulated within the Southern Baptist Convention. As history progressed, the Black Baptist Church eventually embraced the Articles of Faith as an acceptable foundation for doctrinal teaching as well. Even though the theology of the Black Baptist Church is radically different from that of the Southern Baptist Church in many areas; on the subject of basic doctrinal beliefs and tenets of the faith, there is common ground and some mutual agreement.

Perhaps the new calling is for the Black Church to write and create its' own Articles of Faith which are based in the experience and ethos of the Black Church in America. In essence, this book represents commentary and reflections on these Articles of Faith from the perspective of a pastor of a Black Baptist Church. Therefore, the teachings and emphases that emerge from the lessons will have different nuances and will reflect the experience of African-Americans in the Baptist Church of today. Much like the current impressive effort in the development of the African-American Lectionary that is providing guidance and inspiration for Pastors and preachers all over the world, a new collaborative effort involving African-American theologians and Pastors could likewise create a new collection of *African-American Articles of Faith* that capture new doctrinal beliefs based on new questions and organizes them into a meaningful framework that could be embraced by clergy and laity alike.

Since I have now disclosed my own personal faith tradition and paradigm as being black and Baptist, I am keenly aware that some who are from different traditions and paradigms may feel excluded or left out of the dialogue. Each faith tradition and denomination has their own equivalents to the Articles of Faith that serve as their own definitive treasure chests of doctrinal teaching. The use of the Articles of Faith as the foundational framework of teaching and learning in this book reflects my attempt to be transparent with my own theological biases while using the starting place that myself and the congregation that I serve are most familiar with, and in no way should be interpreted as an attempt to *convert* other denominations or faith traditions to the Baptist Faith. All denominations and faith traditions have their own doctrinal teachings in many of the same categories that in some cases are the same, sometimes are similar, and may at times be radically different than those represented in the Articles of Faith. Whatever the case, it is my hope that the topics covered in the presentations that follow will inspire pastors and congregations to have meaningful dialogue on these issues and move them closer to a more comprehensive understanding of their faith, whatever their faith tradition or authoritative doctrinal document may be.

ARTICLES OF FAITH

The Articles of Faith, which should be adopted by Baptist churches at the time of organization:

I. THE SCRIPTURES.

We believe that the Holy Bible was written by men divinely inspired, and is a perfect treasure of heavenly instruction; that it has God for its author, salvation for its end, and truth without any mixture of error for its matter; that it reveals the principles by which God will judge us, and therefore is, and shall remain to the end of the world, the true center of Christian union, and the supreme standard by which all human conduct, creeds, and opinions shall be tried.

II. THE TRUE GOD.

We believe the Scriptures teach that there is one, and only one, living and true God, an infinite, intelligent Spirit, whose name is Jehovah, the Maker and Supreme Ruler of heaven and earth; inexpressibly glorious in holiness, and worthy of all possible honor confidence and love; that in the unity of the Godhead there are three persons, the Father, the Son, and the Holy Ghost; equal in every divine perfection, and executing distinct but harmonious offices in the great work of redemption.

III. THE FALL OF MAN.

We believe the Scriptures teach that Man was created in holiness, under the law of his Maker; but by voluntary transgressions fell from that holy and happy state; in consequence of which all mankind are now sinners, not constraint but choice; being by nature utterly void of that holiness required by the law of God, positively inclined to evil; and therefore under just condemnation to eternal ruin, without defense or excuse.

IV. THE WAY OF SALVATION.

We believe that the Scriptures teach that the salvation of sinners is wholly of grace; through the mediatorial offices of the Son of God;

who by the appointment of the Father, freely took upon him our nature, yet without sin; honored the divine law by his personal obedience, and by his death made a full atonement for our sins; that having risen from the dead, he is now enthroned in heaven; and uniting in his wonderful person the tenderest sympathies with divine perfections, he is in every way qualified to be a suitable, a compassionate, and all-sufficient Saviour.

V. JUSTIFICATION.

We believe the Scriptures teach that the great Gospel blessing which Christ secures to such as believe in him is justification; that justification includes the pardon of sin, and the promise of eternal life on principles of righteousness; that it is bestowed, not in consideration of any works of righteousness which we have done, but solely through faith in the Redeemer's blood; by virtue of which faith his perfect righteousness is freely imputed to us of God; that it brings us into a state of most blessed peace and favor with God, and secures every other blessing needful for time and eternity.

VI. THE FREENESS OF SALVATION.

We believe that the Scriptures teach that the blessings of salvation are made free to all by the Gospel; that it is the immediate duty of all to accept them by cordial, penitent and obedient faith; and that nothing prevents the salvation of the greatest sinner on earth, but his own determined depravity and voluntary rejection of the Gospel; which rejection involves him in an aggravated condemnation.

VII. REGENERATION.

We believe that the Scriptures teach that in order to be saved, sinners must be regenerated, or born again; that regeneration consists in giving a holy disposition to mind that it is effected in a manner above our comprehension by the power of the Holy Spirit in connection with divine truth, so as to secure our voluntary obedience to the Gospel; and that its proper evidence appears in the holy fruits of repentance and faith, and newness of life.

VIII. REPENTANCE AND FAITH.

We believe the Scriptures teach that repentance and faith are sacred duties, and also inseparable graces, wrought in our souls by the regenerating Spirits of God; whereby being deeply convinced of our guilt, danger and helplessness and of the way of salvation by Christ, we turn to God with unfeigned contrition, confession, and supplication for mercy; at the same time heartily receiving the Lord Jesus Christ as our prophet, priest and king, and relying on him alone as the only and all-sufficient Saviour.

IX. GOD'S PURPOSE OF GRACE.

We believe the Scriptures teach that election is the eternal purpose of God, according to which he graciously regenerates, sanctifies and saves sinners; that being perfectly consistent with the free agency of man, it comprehends all the means in connection with the end; that it is a most glorious display of God's sovereign goodness, being infinitely free, wise, holy and unchangeable; that it utterly excludes boasting and promotes humility, love, prayer, praise, trust in God, and active imitation of his free mercy; that it encourages the use of means in the highest degree; that it may be ascertained by its effects in all who truly believe the Gospel; that it is the foundation of Christian assurance; and that to ascertain it with regard to ourselves demands and deserves the utmost diligence.

X. SANCTIFICATION.

We believe the Scriptures teach that Sanctification is the process by which, according to will of God, we are made partakers of his holiness; that it is a progressive work; that it is begun in regeneration; and that it is carried on in the hearts of believers by the presence and power of the Holy Spirit, the Sealer and Comforter, in the continual use of the appointed means especially the word of God, self-examination, self-denial, watchfulness and prayer.

XI. PERSEVERANCE OF SAINTS.

We believe the Scriptures teach that such only are real believers as endure to the end; that their persevering attachment of Christ is the grand mark which distinguishes them from superficial professors; that a special Providence watches over their welfare; and they are kept by the power of God through faith unto salvation.

XII. THE LAW AND GOSPEL.

We believe the Scriptures teach that the Law of God is the eternal and unchangeable rule of his moral government; that it is holy, just and good; and that the inability which the Scriptures ascribe to fallen men to fulfill its precepts, arise entirely from their love of sin; to deliver them from which, and to restore them through a Mediator to unfeigned obedience to the holy Law, is one great end of the Gospel, and of the Means of Grace connected with the establishment of the visible church.

XIII. A GOSPEL CHURCH.

We believe the Scriptures teach that a visible church of Christ is a congregation of baptized believers, associated by covenant in the faith and fellowship of the Gospel; observing the ordinances of Christ; governed by his laws; and exercising the gifts, right, and privileges invested in them by His Word; that its only scriptural officers are Bishops or Pastors, and Deacons whose Qualifications, claims and duties are defined in the Epistles to Timothy and Titus.

XIV. BAPTISM AND THE LORD'S SUPPER.

We believe the Scriptures teach that Christian baptism is the immersion in water of a believer, into the name of the Father, and Son, and Holy Ghost; to show forth in a solemn and beautiful emblem, our faith in crucified, buried, and risen Saviour, with its effect, in our death to sin and resurrection to a new life; that it is prerequisite to the privileges of a church, by the sacred use of bread and wine, are to commemorate together the dying love of Christ; preceded always by solemn self-examination.

XV. THE CHRISTIAN SABBATH.

We believe the Scriptures teach that the first day of the week is the Lord's Day, or Christian Sabbath, and is to be kept sacred to religious purposes, by abstaining from all secular labor and sinful recreations, by the devout observance of all the means of grace, both private and public, and by a preparation for that rest that remaineth for the people of God.

XVI. CIVIL GOVERNMENT.

We believe the Scriptures teach that civil government is of divine appointment, for the interest and good order of human society; and that magistrates are to be prayed for, conscientiously honored and obeyed; except only in things opposed to the will of our Lord Jesus Christ, who is the only Lord of the conscience, and the Prince of the Kings of the earth.

XVII. RIGHTEOUS AND WICKED.

We believe the Scriptures teach that there is a radical and essential difference between the righteous and the wicked; that such only as through faith are justified in the name of the Lord Jesus, and sanctified by the Spirit of our God, are truly righteous in his esteem; while all such as continue in impenitence and unbelief are in his sight wicked, and under the curse; and this distinction holds among men both in and after death.

XVIII. THE WORLD TO COME.

We believe the Scriptures teach that the end of the world is approaching, that at the last day, Christ will descend from heaven, and raise the dead from the grave for final retribution; that a solemn separation will then take place; that the wicked will be adjudged to endless punishment, and the righteous to end- less joy; and that this judgment will fix forever the final state of men in heaven or hell, on principles of righteousness.

THE ARTICLES OF FAITH; *REMIX*
Re-writing and Re-interpreting a classic for today's believer

When those of us who are clergy, theologians and scholars in the church have heretofore written what we consider to be substantive works that contribute to the church's body of knowledge, we tend to often be guilty of being too wordy, overly technical, and often use complex theological language and terminology that the average layperson in the pew would not understand. We often write for the academy or the seminary, and because we know that what we write will be sharply scrutinized and critiqued by our peers, we find ourselves often writing in order to impress other clergy and scholars in order to prove that we have received respectable academic training that is commensurate with the degree that we hold.

The unfortunate casualty of all of this is that we write in ways that are above the heads of most of the laity in churches. So, the average layperson cannot benefit from our work in a practical way. Most often, the people in the pew can't understand or decipher what we are trying to say, let alone use it with any meaningful practical application.

It is with this in mind that I now submit "The Articles of Faith; Remix", which is intended to be a concise, simplified contemporary version of a classic document for today's believer. This is offered as a re-write to an established standard for the purpose of helping today's hearer bridge the gap between the message and substance of the classic and the contemporary, post-modern understanding and language of Christians in my context of ministry, which is the Black Baptist Church.

In today's post-Modern culture especially in the world of hip-hop, when a musical artist does a remix of a classic song that has been around for awhile they are in essence retaining the basic substance of the melody of the song, but using their freedom to improvise around the fringes of the core melody so that they are making the song speak in a new, fresh way. A remix involves the use of new language and new symbols that will add new nuances of meaning for the sake of effective communication. The intent is that hearers who may not have resonated with the melody of the classic song will then hear the remix version that incorporates creativity and expressions that they do resonate with and then be able to embrace the classic song because it speaks to their experience in a new way.

It is in this spirit that I offer this remix of the articles of faith. I believe that these classics have substance and value that will be beneficial to those who don't know them. So to facilitate the introduction between this standard classic and a new generation of hearers, I have re-written and re-interpreted the classic without losing the essence and substance of the message. I pray that God's Spirit will use the remix to speak to today's believers in a new way.

THE ARTICLES OF FAITH *REMIX*
1. THE SCRIPTURES

We believe that the Bible is the ultimate source and authority that determines and defines what we believe and practice in our doctrine; it is the standard for how we are to live both personally and collectively in every area of our daily lives.

The Bible is God's word to us, and God is the author; it reveals God's truth for all of creation without any errors in its content. God used men whom He inspired, motivated and guided to write the Bible and reveal God's nature, God's character and God's plan for the salvation of all of humanity.

2. THE TRUE GOD

We believe that there is only one true God of the universe who is the creator, sustainer and ruler of all of creation. God's identity is revealed to us in the Godhead, which consists of three distinct persons; the Father, the Son, Jesus Christ, and the Holy Spirit. These three persons operate in perfect harmonious unity to accomplish God's will and purposes in the world.

3. THE FALL OF MAN

We believe that God initially created human beings to be in perfect, intimate relationship with God, and therefore were without sin. Unfortunately, man sinned against God and broke that relationship and connection to God. The consequences of that initial sin were severe and caused death to come upon humanity while also revealing a dangerous flaw in human beings; free choice could be used to sin against God, rebel against God's will for us, and to falsely think of ourselves as equal to God.

4. THE WAY OF SALVATION

We believe that God's remedy and provision for human sin is the gift of salvation, which comes by the grace of God and through faith in Jesus Christ, the savior and Son of God. Jesus Christ, who is God in human flesh, took upon Himself the sins of the whole world and died on the cross. Jesus' death paid the price for all of our sins, and His resurrection from the dead makes it possible for us to have new and abundant life free from the penalty of sin.

5. JUSTIFICATION

We believe that when we have faith in the death, burial and resurrection of Jesus Christ, that God justifies us; meaning that God declares us righteous because we are covered by the sacrificial death of Jesus Christ that has paid the price for our sins. In Justification, God declares that we have met His standards of holiness and righteousness because Jesus Christ did it for us and we have accepted Him as Lord of our lives.

6. THE FREENESS OF SALVATION

We believe that God's invitation to salvation through Jesus Christ is available to all people without exception. Anyone who accepts and embraces Jesus Christ as their Lord and Savior in their heart freely receives salvation as a gift from God. The only thing that prevents a person from freely receiving salvation is their own refusal to accept God's invitation.

7. REGENERATION

We believe that when we experience salvation through Jesus

Christ that we are regenerated or "born again". When we truly experience salvation, our nature, our character, our will, and our actions will be changed to be in agreement with the will of God for our lives, and it will also be our desire to grow in this way. Because we have been changed by God, we will change the way we live from now on so that God will be pleased with us.

8. REPENTANCE AND FAITH

We believe that repentance and faith are essential for a Christian to truly live according to God's will. Repentance means that we acknowledge that we are sorry for the sins that we have committed against God, and that we are making an intentional choice to not repeat them, but to change the way we live. We are only able to do this because of our faith in Jesus Christ who empowers us and teaches us how to live for God.

9. GOD'S PURPOSE OF GRACE

We believe that Christians who are in Christ are considered to be chosen, predestined, or part of the elect by God, because Jesus Christ has given our life new meaning, new purpose and a new destination. We are only in Christ by the grace of God, and therefore all of the new possibilities and purposes that come into our lives because of our relationship with Jesus Christ are gifts from God. God's purpose of grace is to bring us back into a right relationship with Him as it existed before sin affected humanity; it is God working on our behalf and bringing us into His will for us. It is a precious gift that we could never earn for ourselves.

10. SANCTIFICATION

We believe that once we experience salvation, God begins a process in our hearts called sanctification that is intended to make us holy, just as God is holy. Although salvation is instantaneous; sanctification is a process by which God makes us holy inwardly in our hearts and outwardly in our actions. God accomplishes this process in us through the presence and power of the Holy Spirit, by teaching us in the bible, and by communicating with us through our prayer lives.

11. PERSEVERANCE OF SAINTS

We believe that when we experience truly authentic salvation from God through Jesus Christ, that it is a reality that endures and lasts not just until the end of our lives, but until the end of time when Jesus comes back to judge the world. Real saints who have truly been born again endure to the end, and cannot and do not lose their salvation because it is a gift from God and it is in God's hands. While there may be those who are falsely professing to know Jesus, whose religion will not endure; the true saints of God are securely kept by the grace of God and sealed until the day of redemption by the Holy Spirit.

12. THE LAW AND GOSPEL

We believe that the laws of God as revealed in the bible are holy, just and good; and that human beings are incapable of fully obeying God's laws on our own. We need the blessings of the Gospel of Jesus Christ to help us to fulfill God's laws. In essence, the law of

God points out our need for the Gospel in our lives because it exposes our sins. What we cannot do through human effort, Jesus Christ does for us in the Gospel story; therefore, law and Gospel go hand in hand for Christians.

13. A GOSPEL CHURCH

We believe that God established the church as the body of Christ for the mutual edification and nurturing of Christians, and that it consists of baptized believers who are in relationship with God and one another; and are called by God to carry the Gospel into the world in both word and deed. The church belongs to God, and it is governed by the Holy Bible in all matters and methods. The only official servant-leaders of the church are the Pastors or Bishops, and the Deacons; whose duties, qualifications and functions are described in the bible.

14. BAPTISM AND THE LORD'S SUPPER

We believe that baptism is an ordinance that we submit to as an outward sign or witness that we have experienced salvation through Jesus Christ. Baptism is done by immersion of the believer in water in the name of the Father, and of the Son and of the Holy Spirit; it signifies our death to sin and our resurrection to new life in Jesus Christ.

We further believe that the Lord's Supper is an ordinance that we practice in the church that commemorates the death, burial and resurrection of Jesus Christ. The bread signifies the body of our Lord Jesus Christ, which He gave to die on the cross of Calvary; and the cup signifies His blood, which was shed at Calvary for the forgiveness of our sins. Whenever we do it, it is done in remembrance of Jesus Christ.

15. THE CHRISTIAN SABBATH

We believe that the first day of the week, Sunday, is the Christian Sabbath or the Lord's Day. The Christian Sabbath is a holy day because it is the day that Jesus was resurrected from the dead. It has its roots in the Old Testament Sabbath, and should therefore be observed as a day of worship, rest and meditation on our life with God and the church both privately and publicly.

16. CIVIL GOVERNMENT

We believe that governmental officials on all levels are supposed to be servants who are appointed and affirmed by God to serve and maintain order in human society. God is sovereign over all government leaders, and Christians should pray for those who occupy political positions of leadership on all levels. Christians are both heavenly citizens and earthly citizens; and just as we are accountable for following God's law, we should also respect the law of the land. If the law of the land is unjust, then we must work as agents of change and transformation empowered by God to change the law and the positions of governmental leaders as appropriate.

17. RIGHTEOUS AND WICKED

We believe that there is a distinct difference between good and evil in the world. There are righteous people and wicked people in the world, and there is also a heaven and a hell. God is the one who has authority to judge between the two, and the difference is whether or not a person has a relationship or connection with God. Those who reject God and rebel against God's will are the wicked, and their works are evil in the world because they are ungodly and against the message of the Gospel of Jesus Christ. A time will come when God will judge between the righteous and wicked, and each will receive the reward or consequences associated with the life they have lived in this world.

18. THE WORLD TO COME

We believe that God has a time and a way for this world as we know it to come to an end and give way to God's new creation of a new heaven and a new earth. No man knows the day or the hour when this time will come, that knowledge is held by God alone. It is our responsibility to live each day in anticipation of God's plan and using the time responsibly to spread God's message throughout the world. When this new world comes, Jesus will return as a King to judge the world and those in it, and God will reign forever.

Chapter 1

The Scriptures and Our True God

Article I. THE SCRIPTURES

Jeremiah 15:16, 2 Timothy 3:16-17, John 1:1-14

The Scriptures:

The traditional interpretation of the Articles of Faith:

We believe that the Holy Bible was written by men divinely inspired, and is a perfect treasure of heavenly instruction; that it has God for its author, salvation for its end, and truth without any mixture of error for its matter; that it reveals the principles by which God will judge us, and therefore is, and shall remain to the end of the world, the true center of Christian union, and the supreme standard by which all human conduct, creeds, and opinions shall be tried.

REMIXED:

We believe that the Bible is the ultimate source and authority that determines and defines what we believe and practice in our doctrine; it is the standard for how we are to live both personally and collectively in every area of our daily lives.

The Bible is God's word to us, and God is the author; it reveals God's truth for all of creation without any errors in its content. God used men whom He inspired, motivated and guided to write the Bible and reveal God's nature, God's character and God's plan for the salvation of all of humanity.

Of all of the places where a foundational doctrinal statement of a church or denomination could begin, ours begins with the scriptures.

This is clearly an indication that we are a church that believes that scripture is authoritative and important for us as we live lives of faith. First and foremost, we are people who believe in the scriptures, the bible, because it is the Word of God in written form. We believe that the Bible is relevant and authoritative for all areas of our lives as we live for God. We are "people of the book", and we believe that, in the 66 books of the Old and New Testament, God has revealed Himself to humanity and communicates to us His will and purpose.

In this contemporary post-modern culture that we now live in, the Bible is thought by some to be simply "helpful suggestions" that humanity can accept or reject. But we in the church believe that the Bible is the word of God, and that it is God's Design and Will for how we should live our lives. We are committed to living according to the scriptures as faithfully as we can. Among the important doctrinal teachings in this article of faith are the following:

The Inspiration of the Bible:

We believe that the Bible was written by men who were divinely inspired by God's Holy Spirit to write as God moved on their hearts. While men did the physical writing, we believe that God is the actual author of the Bible. While men are limited because of their finite experience and humanity, God is able to move on the hearts of finite beings and use them to communicate infinite truths about God's self. While there are many different human writers who contributed to the physical writing of the Bible, over the test of time, cultures and other human differences, the message of the Bible is consistently clear in presenting God and God's intent for humanity. God communicates to us through the channels of human experience and human expression from various walks of life, but the author is still God. It is God who inspired men to write the scriptures in ways that we can understand. No one human writer wrote EVERYTHING that there is to know about God, rather God used each writer to give us a piece of revelation about God. Hence, we must read the whole bible to be exposed to the many ways that God inspired the human writers.

The Content of the Bible:

We believe that the Scripture has "*salvation as its end, and truth without any mixture of error for its' matter.*" So, we believe that God's intent in Scripture is to reveal His means and provisions for salvation of humanity and all of creation. The Scriptures contain accounts of the saving power of God in the history of mankind since the beginning of time. Hence, the content of the Bible is concerned with Salvation, and it constantly points to Salvation as God's ultimate will for humanity and creation.

We further believe that the Scripture does not have errors in it. This means that the content and principles that God communicates with us in the Bible are inerrant, meaning that there are no mistakes in them. Much has been said about the mistakes that human beings make, and if they are in the process, then there must be some errors. But we must remember that the scripture is essentially a theological book about God, not a textbook in an academic discipline. The principles communicated about God in scripture are always right.

Scripture only makes sense when we read it with a Christological focus.

The Interpretation of the Bible:

We believe that the best and only way to interpret scripture is through the lens of Jesus Christ. That is, for any scripture Old or New Testament, we look at it in light of what we know about Jesus. Jesus is the Word that became flesh, and He is the fullest and most complete living revelation of God known to the world. Scripture only makes sense when we read it with a Christological focus.

Article II. THE TRUE GOD

Genesis 1:1; Exodus 3:14, 6:2-3; Deuteronomy 6:4; Jeremiah 10:10; John 4:24; 1 Corinthians 8:6; Ephesians 4:6; Colossians 2:6-10; 1Timothy 1:17; 1 John 5:7

The True God:

The traditional interpretation of the Articles of Faith:

We believe the Scriptures teach that there is one, and only one, living and true God, an infinite, intelligent Spirit, whose name is Jehovah, the Maker and Supreme Ruler of heaven and earth; inexpressibly glorious in holiness, and worthy of all possible honor confidence and love; that in the unity of the Godhead there are three persons, the Father, the Son, and the Holy Ghost; equal in every divine perfection, and executing distinct but harmonious offices in the great work of redemption.

REMIXED:

We believe that there is only one true God of the universe who is the creator, sustainer and ruler of all of creation. God's identity is revealed to us in the Godhead, which consists of three distinct persons; the Father, the Son, Jesus Christ, and the Holy Spirit. These three persons operate in perfect harmonious unity to accomplish God's will and purposes in the world.

Notice that all of the articles of faith after the first one all begin with the words *"we believe that the scriptures teach…"* or something very close to that wording. So, we can see that the scripture forms the basis of all of our doctrinal belief and teaching. Since we learned that the scriptures have God as the author, then it follows that after we establish a proper understanding of scripture then the next logical question would be, *"who is God?"* We see from this article of faith that we believe that there is one and only one true God who is an infinite, intelligent Spirit and whose name is Jehovah. We believe that the scripture teaches us that God is the supreme ruler of heaven and earth, and that He made all of creation. We also see that God reveals Himself in a "Trinitarian" way. God is Father, Son and Holy Spirit and the three are in perfect unity with one another operating harmoniously and distinctly in God's plan of redemption. The Trinity does NOT mean three different gods! We worship one God in three persons of the trinity who operate in perfect unity. While this seems to be strange to some, one must acknowledge that God is infinite and is there- fore beyond our human finite understanding of life and reality. Because of this, we can never fully *define* God! The best we human beings can do is to *describe* God, and our description is based on what God chooses to reveal to us about Himself and humanity's experience with Him, as our God. That is why the Bible is so critical to our understanding of God, since it contains stories about God's interaction with human beings throughout human history. Among all of the important things to be known about the true God, this article highlights the following:

The Names of God:

In Exodus 6:3 we see God referring to His name "Jehovah". However, scripture also reveals several other names of God which include: *Elohim*, which means God; *Adonai*, which means Lord; and several other compounds of Jehovah which describe God's activity in a given situation. In the New Testament, the word *Theos* is used for God, and *Kurious* means Lord in the Greek text. Additionally, there are numerous other titles given to Jesus, which include Son of God, Son of Man, Christ, Word, Master, Messiah, etc... All of the various names of God reflect descriptions regarding how God worked with human beings in various situations, and how human beings responded to God, usually through worship, praise, or a commitment to a Godly way of life. It is interesting to note that the name "Jesus" means *Jehovah is salvation*. The name Jehovah comes from the *Tetragrammaton* in the Old Testament, which is, to be clear, the unpronounceable name for God in the Hebrew text of the Bible. Even in scripture, Jews would not say it because they believed it was holy. Jehovah then is an approximate transliteration from the Hebrew to English, but we do not know the actual pronunciation.

__The Trinity does NOT mean three different gods!__
__We worship one God in three persons of__
__the trinity who operate in perfect unity.__

The Attributes of God:

The Scripture teaches us that God has certain attributes that are consistent throughout all creation and history. God has both natural *attributes* and *moral* attributes that we see in scripture.

God's *natural attributes* are:
- *Self existence,* God is an eternal being and He exists because of Himself
- *Immutability,* God does not change His character, nature or purpose
- *Omnipresence,* God is present everywhere at all times in all of creation
- *Immensity,* God is superior to space, He is not bound by space or time
- *Eternity,* God has no beginning or ending; past, present and future are in His hands
- *Omniscience,* God knows all things, He has all knowledge
- *Omnipotence,* God has all power, He can do anything He wants to.

God's *moral attributes* are:
- *Holiness,* God's supreme moral excellence
- *Righteousness,* God's nature affirms right over wrong, and good over evil
- *Truth,* God is the source and grounds for all truth in all of creation
- *Love,* God is Love, unconditional pure devoted love that has absolute loyalty

The Trinitarian Nature of God:

While the actual word "trinity" does not appear in the bible, we acknowledge that the bible does speak in "Trinitarian" language about God. We know that, in the Old Testament, the word *elohim*, which is a name for God, is in the plural form. Additionally, we hear God speaking in the plural voice by saying "let *us* make man in our image…"(Genesis 1:26) and also "whom shall I send and who will go for us"(Isaiah 6:8). Another compelling argument occurs in Colossians 2:9 that speaks about the "Godhead" dwelling in Jesus Christ bodily. 1 John 5:7 is also a definitive statement about the Trinitarian nature of God. Additionally, we cannot ignore that Jesus himself speaks in Trinitarian language in Matthew 28:19 and several other places in the scripture.

We believe that the Father, Son, and Holy Spirit make up the Trinity, and that One God reveals Himself in this Trinitarian way. We believe that all three persons of the trinity operate in perfect unity and harmony with each other. **God, the Father** is the reigning providential authority over all of creation and the universe and all who dwell in it. The Father directs the flow of human history according to His redemptive plan.

God, the Son, Jesus is the word made flesh. He is the incarnation of God who came to earth as the fullest and most complete revelation of God in bodily form. Jesus came as our savior to die on the cross for the salvation and redemption of the whole world. He arose from the dead on the third day, according to the scriptures with all power in His hand. He is the standard by which all scripture should be read. He is King of Kings, and is coming back to judge the world.

God, the Holy Spirit is the living active power of God in the world. He conceived Jesus in the Virgin Mary. He reveals God to humanity, works through humanity, convicts us of sin, lives within us and comforts us. The Holy Spirit also gives us spiritual gifts as people of God.

Reader's Remix:
Real-life Reflections on Chapter One

The Scriptures and One True God. At first glance, these are easy concepts to digest. In application to daily life, however, they can be a bit more challenging to implement, follow, and adhere to – particularly in today's world when the challenges are so great and the universal realities often so brutal.

> *Now we know what we should believe in Scripture and about our God; how do we move forward and execute our plan?*

Now, plainly spoken, we have examined perhaps the most straightforward of the Articles of Faith – our scriptures with which we should all be familiar – and our God, who we know inherently. We have examined them "remixed" and brought them to a human and day-to-day level of understanding and application. In this way, they are easy to handle; we read them, we digest them, and we think about how to apply this newfound or reviewed information to our lives. And, here, of course, is where it gets tricky. How, exactly, do we do this?

In simple terms, I can tell you that you need to reread your Bible – become familiar with God's Written Word. I can tell you to go forth and talk about your God and your belief in Him. I can also tell you that it is you who needs to stay vigilant and continue your education as a Christian and as a member of your church. Is it enough, however, to love God and simply know that the scriptures are His Written Word, or is it better, more practical, even, to realize that to communicate your faith and your understanding of God and Scriptures, you need to study and live His Word?

Remember that newspaper article we referenced at the beginning of the book – before we closely examined the first of our Articles of Faith? That article is our wake-up call. We need to live our faith and understand our place in this world. The Articles of Faith will serve as our guidebook at times, but it is us, the human element in any church, who must carry on God's Word. We have already established that the Bible was written by men who were communicating God's absolute word – His design for us in life. Why, then, can we not manage to do the same? It is our mission, and this book will serve as guide for providing the right background in establishing and feeding this commitment.

Regarding scripture and our role in applying the Word of God, specifically, to our daily lives, I have to be frank. We, as Christians, DO need to understand what we are reading, what we are taught, and, of course, what we are hearing from the pulpit on Sunday. Do we always understand the message, even the King James text and language in these readings? Again, it is time to be frank; ask yourselves if you really hear the message - understand what is being asked of us as Christians. We have to believe God's Word; therefore, we need to, not only understand it, we need to truly digest it, live it, and make sure that it is, in turn, being taught and spread throughout our communities. When we first discussed the premise of being "raised in the church" earlier in the book, we could all recall Sunday services, Christian education classes, social gatherings and dinners held at the local church, and the whole community rallying together when someone was sick, in need, or even had something to celebrate. The church was one big family; all with the same belief system and ethics regarding imparting that belief system onto the younger members of the church. By reading our scripture and truly testing ourselves to understand what Jesus lived, what God was and is trying to tell us, and what is being asked of us all these years later as Christians, we can effectively teach our children, recruit the nonbelievers, and educate the community, Christians and agnostics alike.

Further, in understanding our God through the Trinity, we can really feel Him - we can truly empathize with Jesus our Savior - and we can accept the Holy Spirit into our lives on a daily basis. Again, this little nuance - keeping the Trinity in mind and truly making ourselves aware of God in all His manifestations and under all His names - can allow us to emerge as leaders or nurturers, if you will. We need to stand and give praise to God daily. Our food, our livelihood, our beautiful families are all through the Grace of God. The loss of our loved ones, the trials that life throws our way, and the acceptance that life is not always perfect is by God's Hand too. How does this come about? Why does He give us such glory and, on the other hand, such pain? If we know Him - trust Him - believe in Him inherently, we can reach a level of faith that will further His presence in the church and in the community. As the core of our belief system, breaking down and understanding our Articles of Faith can do that.

Even the most faithful will question God in times of sorrow or great pain. Why did I lose this person? How can I get through this difficult time? Why has this happened to me? And, truthfully, in times of job loss, illness, money trouble, addiction, or even just moments of soul-searching during which it seems there will be no answers – no direction to your life – no help – God is there, and we can reference His Word any time we need to be re-bolstered in our attempts to lead a faithful life or rejuvenated in our daily trials and tribulations.

In today's world, finances are often difficult – war throughout the world is prevalent – and, like generations before us, we are beset with natural disasters that seem to affect the most vulnerable in society – those already suffering with disease or financial hardship. Even when we don't feel the pain, personally, it is hard to come to terms with why these things happen.

When we come to terms with the fact that God does have a plan, and that we can draw strength from the examples set forth in the Bible, we can, then, handle what is sent our way – we can empathize with and help those in need – we can shoulder any burden and any joy that we are meant to receive.

Today is different than our parents' generation – our grandparents' and great-grandparents' generations. In the midst of a world in turmoil (at times), we also have great opportunities; we can do or be anything we want to – in most cases. Education is available – travel is easier – being connected across the miles is more feasible. We see ordinary people becoming famous, daily, and we hear constantly about successful entrepreneurs or personalities all over the world. We can be whoever we want to be; we can, presumably, do whatever we want to do.

When we come to terms with the fact that God does have a plan, and that we can draw strength from the examples set forth in the Bible, we can, then, handle what is sent our way – we can empathize with and help those in need – we can shoulder any burden and any joy that we are meant to receive. Will we chose God's way in all situations? We should. We know we should, but … do we always follow that path? Again, given the Scriptures and our daily interactions with God, we can make this our path.

Chapter 2

The Fall of Man, Salvation, and Justification

Article III. THE FALL OF MAN
Genesis 2:25, 3:1-24; Psalm 51:5; Romans 5:12-21; Romans 6:23; 1 Corinthians 15:22

The Fall of Man:
The traditional interpretation of the Articles of Faith:
We believe the Scriptures teach that Man was created in holiness, under the law of his Maker; but by voluntary transgressions fell from that holy and happy state; in consequence of which all mankind are now sinners, not constraint but choice; being by nature utterly void of that holiness required by the law of God, positively inclined to evil; and therefore under just condemnation to eternal ruin, without defense or excuse.

REMIXED:
We believe that God initially created human beings to be in perfect, intimate relationship with God, and therefore were without sin. Unfortunately, man sinned against God and broke that relationship and connection to God. The consequences of that initial sin were severe and caused death to come upon humanity while also revealing a dangerous flaw in human beings; free choice could be used to sin against God, rebel against God's will for us, and to falsely think of ourselves as equal to God.

This article of our faith is essential to our understanding regarding *why* we need God in our lives. This doctrine teaches us *how* human beings came to a state of total depravity and sinfulness in our existence and further points to why we need Jesus Christ our Savior. In order for people to understand the necessity of God in our lives, we must first realize what is wrong in our respective lives, and then acknowledge that we cannot fix it ourselves, and then realize that only God can save us, fix us, and redeem us through Jesus Christ.

What is traditionally known as *"The Fall of Man"* is the biblical account of how sin entered into the world and, thus, changed humanity from our original state of innocence and an unbroken relationship with God. Sin is defined as willful disobedience or rebellion against God. Sin breaks our fellowship with God and paints a picture of us that is not consistent with the image that God had in mind for us. Satan, the adversary, is always interested in tempting us and persuading us to not live up to the image of God because we are the crown of God's creation! When Satan tempts us to sin, and we yield, we are breaking the fellowship we have with God and denying the identity and purpose for which God made us. We are, in essence, worshipping self instead of God. Satan always makes temptation seem more pleasing than God's way, but the tragedy is that, once we fall into this trap, we cannot fix it or make it right ourselves, and we have rightfully put ourselves in a position of being judged by God's standards of holiness and righteousness. This event with Adam and Eve was truly a *fall* because it is the introduction of sin into the world, and all of humanity inherited this sin nature and the consequences of living with it. Consider the following:

Humanity's state prior to the Fall

Before the Fall in Genesis chapter 3, Scripture records that God had made all of creation and then made man and woman, both the crown of God's entire creation. They were in a state of pure relationship and fellowship with God. God had provided EVERYTHING that they needed and had given them authority and dominion over creation. God had even given them each other. They were ONE! Adam said that Eve was *"bone of his bones and flesh of his flesh"*. They were a unified couple living together in paradise. They had perfect unity with God and with each other. God had given them provision for all of their needs, and had also given them His law for them to obey. Genesis 2:17 clearly states that they were not to eat of the Tree of the Knowledge of Good and Evil. As long as they followed God's commands, they were in a perfect state of innocence and fellowship with God and each other. They were naked, but unashamed in a perfect state of innocence. This is a picture of what God's initial plan and desire for humanity was prior to the fall. All was well the way God created humanity, but unfortunately, God's plan was not followed as it was designed.

How the Fall happened

The Bible records how Satan, in the form of a serpent, enters the scene and tempts Eve and Adam to sin against the command of God. In general, Satan tempted them in three particular ways: Using ambition, aesthetics, and physical need.

To this day, temptation pulls us away from obedience to God's commands by appealing to our appetites for things that we secretly desire. *Ambition* involves our longing to be something that we aspire to be for our own ego, but is not God's will for us. *Aesthetics* means that something looks so good to us that we desire to possess it and control it, again to satisfy self. And *physical* temptation means that we are drawn by strong desires in our flesh, which overcome our commitment to obey God. We essentially let our flesh dictate our actions rather than our faith. Sin may happen with the urging of temptation, but it is ultimately caused by our choice. Sin is a willful choice to purposely, either by omission or commission, disobey or rebel against what God has said. This was the first sin of humanity in God's creation. Humanity had decided to not reflect the image of God that they had been created in. As a result, Adam and Eve and all of humanity and creation came under the judgment of God and died in that moment. The death was spiritual and would manifest itself physically as well; basically, separation from God results in both ultimate physical and spiritual death. Further, death is separation from God, and it is caused by sin.

The Consequences of the Fall

As to be expected, the consequences of the *Fall of Man* were very costly. Some of these consequences include:

- **A Loss of innocence**. Adam and Eve suddenly knew that they were naked, and they were ashamed.
- **A Loss of Unity and tendency to blame each other.** Adam blamed Eve and tried to suggest that God giving her to him was the cause! After all, sin has the potential to tear apart meaningful relationships between human beings, which causes us to point fingers of blame at each other even in our own lives.
- **A sin nature that leads to death is passed onto all humanity**. Once innocence is lost, it cannot be recovered as if it

never happened. The sinful nature is passed on from person to person and from generation to generation. We are born in sin and shaped in iniquity. All human beings inherit and learn a sin nature that is prone to disobey God.

• A Curse from God on the serpent, Eve, and Adam that includes:
- Dismissal from the paradise in the Garden of Eden
- Hard work and labor
- Pain and sorrow
- Hierarchical relationships based on power, oppression and authority instead of unity and fellowship.

Article IV. THE WAY OF SALVATION

John 3:16-17; 2 Corinthians 5:17-21; Hebrews 9:11-15; Ephesians 2:1-10; Romans 10:1-10

The Way of Salvation:

The traditional interpretation of the Articles of Faith:

We believe that the Scriptures teach that the salvation of sinners is wholly of grace; through the mediatorial offices of the Son of God; who by the appointment of the Father, freely took upon him our nature, yet without sin; honored the divine law by his personal obedience, and by his death made a full atonement for our sins; that having risen from the dead, he is now enthroned in heaven; and uniting in his wonderful person the tenderest sympathies with divine perfections, he is in every way qualified to be a suitable, a compassionate, and all-sufficient Saviour.

REMIXED:

We believe that God's remedy and provision for human sin is the gift of salvation, which comes by the grace of God and through faith in Jesus Christ, the savior and Son of God. Jesus Christ, who is God in human flesh, took upon Himself the sins of the whole world and died on the cross. Jesus' death paid the price for all of our sins, and His resurrection from the dead makes it possible for us to have new and abundant life free from the penalty of sin.

What does it really mean when we say that we are "*saved*"? This is language that is often used in and about the Christian church but, rarely, is it fully understood by those who hear it. In its simplest sense, to be saved means that someone was in a predicament where death, destruction and danger were imminent if they had not already happened. There must be some- thing that a person is saved *from*, and generally whatever it is, it was not for his or her own good. So, when we are faced with situations of definite destruction, danger and death, and we are rescued from the situation, we can then say that we have been *saved* from the impending consequences of what was about to destroy us. The person who saved us is called a *Savior*, and the act that he or she accomplished for us is called *salvation*. It is also referred to as redemption or being redeemed.

In this doctrinal teaching, we see how Jesus is our savior, and that we are saved from the death and destruction that resulted from the *Fall of Man*. The whole activity of Jesus dying on the cross for our sins and rising on the third day is God's way of Salvation that is available to all who accept the Lord Jesus Christ as their Savior and believe in Him by faith. It was never God's intention for humanity to fall into sin like we did in the Garden of Eden. But since it happened, God also made provision for us to be put back into a life-giving relationship with God through Jesus Christ. Our ever-lasting relationship with Jesus Christ is pure evidence of that provision.

How God provides Salvation

It is important for us to remember that the way of salvation is God's plan and remedy to undo the damage that was done to humanity and creation because of the Fall of Man. Since humanity failed and sinned in the first Adam, God sent a second Adam, who is Jesus Christ; Biblical fact proves the former to us – the Articles of Faith prove the latter. In fact, God took upon Himself human form and flesh. He was human like we are and, unlike the first Adam, Jesus lived without any sin. Since Jesus had no sin Himself, His death was for our sins, the sins of the whole world. So, in essence, God was in Jesus Christ reconciling the world to Himself. Where humanity fell short, God took it upon Himself to live a life that is totally committed to God and completely free from sin for us. Through the death, burial, resurrection and ascension of Jesus Christ; God saved us from the condemnation of sin that came from the fall. God saved us from eternal separation from God, death and hell. God redeemed us - as well as all of creation - and helps us to regain the status with God that we had before the fall, which was based in trust and love.

How humanity gets Salvation

We are saved by Grace through Faith. It is not because of our works or anything that we do to earn salvation like good deeds in life or through the church. Grace literally means "gift", so, literally, salvation comes to us as God's free gift when we confess with our mouth and believe in our heart that the salvation work of Jesus Christ is real. Confession, faith and belief are all what we do in response to this awesome invitation that God extends to us in the plan of Salvation. We don't earn salvation; we don't even get ourselves ready for salvation. It is, instead, a free gift from God, and no one controls who is or is not saved. It is a gift of God that is made available to the whole world. God depends on those of us who are in the church to be His witnesses in the world and to tell others about this important invitation that God has made possible for us through Jesus Christ. There is nothing that we can do to control, manipulate, earn, dictate, or regulate salvation. It is strictly in the hands of God because Jesus paid the ultimate price in death, and this has become the whole price for our salvation. That's why we are so thankful to God, because Jesus did it for us and we could never have done it for ourselves. No matter how hard we try, we could not live sinless like Jesus did. God would have been justified in just destroying all humanity and all creation for our sins, but He loved us so much that He made our salvation and redemption possible through Jesus Christ. This is

His gift to us, and we should receive it humbly, joyously and thankfully. Our proper response should be to gladly give our lives back to God, totally committed to His will and His way. After all, if it were not for Him, our lives and our souls would be lost.

> *After all, if it were not for Him, our lives and our souls would be lost.*

What humanity gets from Salvation

The death of Jesus was an atoning death. That means that it paid the debt that humanity owed because of sin. If the wages of sin are death, then wherever there is sin, death is the result. Remember that death is separation from God. When Jesus died for us, He fulfilled that debt. He died in our place, and then conquered death itself by rising on resurrection day. So because Jesus paid the debt for humanity and conquered death, He is our second Adam – our forerunner of a "new" humanity who is committed to God as God originally intended humans to be - and He returns us to our relationship and status with God that humanity enjoyed before the *Fall of Man*. We are declared righteous by God when we are covered by the salvation that God provided through the atoning death of Jesus Christ. Certainly, we have sinned in our lives. When we confess our sins and God forgives us, God sees that we are covered by the blood of Jesus or atoned for and reconciled to God, and we are declared righteous because the debt has been already paid. What a blessing from God! We are blessed in ways that we don't deserve, with gifts that we don't deserve, all because God loves us so much. Thank God for Jesus! Let us commit ourselves to Him completely. This is how we follow the Articles of Faith.

Article V. JUSTIFICATION
Genesis 15:1-6, Romans 3:20-28, Romans 4:1-8, 25; Romans 5:1-2, 9

Justification:
The traditional interpretation of the Articles of Faith:
We believe the Scriptures teach that the great Gospel blessing

which Christ secures to such as believe in him is justification; that justification includes the pardon of sin, and the promise of eternal life on principles of righteousness; that it is bestowed, not in consideration of any works of righteousness which we have done, but solely through faith in the Redeemer's blood; by virtue of which faith his perfect righteousness is freely imputed to us of God; that it brings us into a state of most blessed peace and favor with God, and secures every other blessing needful for time and eternity.

REMIXED:

We believe that when we have faith in the death, burial and resurrection of Jesus Christ, that God justifies us; meaning that God declares us righteous because we are covered by the sacrificial death of Jesus Christ that has paid the price for our sins. In Justification, God declares that we have met His standards of holiness and righteousness because Jesus Christ did it for us and we have accepted Him as Lord of our lives.

The term "justification" is a legal term that refers to the act of pronouncing someone righteous and/or acquitted from being guilty. As we see in this doctrinal teaching, however, justification is a blessing that is bestowed on us by God because of our faith in God and God's act of salvation in Jesus Christ. Our works have nothing to do with whether or not we are justified; rather, our works are subsequent evidence that we *have been* justified by God. Not only does God forgive our sins and pay the price for our sins, but He then also declares us to be righteous in His sight because we accept Jesus Christ as our savior by faith. Justification is the means by which God declares that we have met His standards of holiness and righteousness. The miracle of Christianity is that we did not do anything to make this possible. Jesus Christ did it all, and we accept God's invitation to this justification by faith.

What is required of us in this is that we believe God and have authentic faith in God. When God sees our authentic faith, He counts it as righteousness for us as he did in the case of Abraham (Genesis 15:6). In the Old Testament, notice that Abraham has no concrete evidence to prove why he should believe God, yet there is something within him that enables him to truly believe God. The scripture then says that God counted it as righteousness for Abraham. That is true faith that leads to our justification. We, too, must believe God and have faith even when we may not have evidence to support it. God will see our faith and honor it.

One of the great sins of humanity is the sin of unbelief. Where there is unbelief or lack of faith, the full extent of the blessings of God cannot be realized because there will always be a human temptation to think that our blessings are as a result of something that we have done. We feel that we should be rewarded for good behavior and punished for bad behavior. In fact, this example of Abraham being declared righteous by God in the Old Testament is written to make a persuasive argument in the early church that Justification is a gift from God based on faith not works – not good or bad behavior – but entirely God's Will and God's Grace. When Jews felt that they were spiritually superior to Gentiles, Paul masterfully pointed out that this declaration by God on Abraham happened *before* the nation of Israel existed and *before* Abraham was ever circumcised; therefore, the blessing and promise of God is not about cultural heritage, religious rituals or any other works. It is solely based on our faith and belief in God. Faith is absolutely necessary in order to be justified by God. Faith gets God's attention. The reality of being justified by God is important because of the following:

1) We have Peace with God.

When we receive justification, God, Himself, declares us righteous. Therefore, we are in a right relationship with God because Jesus has made it possible for us to meet His standards of holiness and righteousness. If it had not been for Jesus, we could have never attained a state of being at peace with God. We would always be in a broken, dysfunctional relationship because of the fall and sin. But now, God, Himself, makes it possible for us to have peace with Him.

2) We have Access to God.

When God justifies us, the peace with God that we are blessed with opens the door of access to God. He is our source of joy and hope. Things that we used to rely on the world to give us are no longer our priority. We can now boldly go to God's throne of grace in prayer and make our petitions known to Him because He has declared us righteous before Himself. Sin breaks the relationship and access, but justification restores it to where God initially intended it to be.

3) We are saved from the Wrath of God.

As unpopular as it may be to say in our society now, sin has consequences. The bible teaches that the wages of sin is, ultimately, death. And, additionally, there are other consequences to sinful actions that affect us in daily living aside from being separated from God in death and sin. When we receive justification from God and God declares us righteous, then we are saved from the wrath and judgment of God because the sacrifice of Jesus is covering us. If it were not for Jesus, we would have no cover to shield us from the wrath of a Holy God. But because we accept Jesus Christ by faith, when God looks at us, He sees the covering of the blood of Jesus – his death - which pays the debt. So instead of receiving wrath, we are declared righteous because of Jesus. That is why we are so thankful for Jesus Christ. Without Him we could never be justified because there is nothing we could have done to earn it.

Reader's Remix:
Real-life Reflectionson Chapter Two

So, we've learned that acceptance of God's grace and will is the key to our freedom from sin. Simply put, Jesus died so that we could be saved and live in God's grace. Though we will constantly struggle with sin, we can receive salvation, and we can be redeemed.

More difficult to understand is the concept that peace, access to God, and even freedom from His wrath is attainable with simple faith. We don't need to do anything – we don't need to put ourselves out at all – because Jesus, our Savior, has already done that. We need to believe and serve God, and his ultimate gift to us will be unconditional love and acceptance. This is an often hard to find deal in today's tricky world. Accept it – live it – and move on. Only in that way will living by these Articles of Faith make sense on a daily basis – on a level outside of church and beyond traditional worship – into our daily disciplines and activities.

The Fall of Man, Salvation and Justification are some heady concepts by which we are told to live. Certainly, we are all familiar with The Fall of Man and Jesus' great sacrifice for us. We know that Salvation is possible – as well as Justification. Do we really know, however, just how much effort receiving the gift of salvation may be? Do we truly understand that it takes commitment and consistency? Do we also realize that it takes a considerable amount of faith, intelligence, and monthly, weekly – even daily – affirmations regarding who we are as Christians.

Can you talk to another about your faith? Can you accept, inherently, that Jesus died for your sins? Can you accept the fact that with some love, some fortitude, and some changes in your life, you can receive salvation?

How do we prepare ourselves for one of God's greatest gifts? Again, as we established earlier, in this world of opportunity and challenge, are we able to pause, reflect, and execute a plan that will bring us to God?

It is never too late to take that pause – stop while we're trying that fancy new restaurant – reflect while we attend a friend's wedding – reach out to others as we walk our path to work daily – and ... make sure that we are worthy of the salvation and the justification waiting for us in God's loving embrace.

Chapter 3

Understanding the Freeness of Salvation and Regeneration

Article VI. THE FREENESS OF SALVATION

John 3:14-18, Romans 10:8-13, Galatians 3:26-29, 1 Timothy 1:9-16

The traditional interpretation of the Articles of Faith:

We believe that the Scriptures teach that the blessings of salvation are made free to all by the Gospel; that it is the immediate duty of all to accept them by cordial, penitent and obedient faith; and that nothing prevents the salvation of the greatest sinner on earth, but his own determined depravity and voluntary rejection of the Gospel; which rejection involves him in an aggravated condemnation.

REMIXED:

We believe that God's invitation to salvation through Jesus Christ is available to all people without exception. Anyone who accepts and embraces Jesus Christ as their Lord and Savior in their heart freely receives salvation as a gift from God. The only thing that prevents a person from freely receiving salvation is their own refusal to accept God's invitation.

Salvation is free! However, as we have learned in the doctrine of the way of salvation, just because it is free does not mean it is *cheap*! Salvation is a free gift from God that God extends as an invitation to all humanity. Scripture teaches that it is God's desire that all humanity would be saved, and God has provided the means for it. Indeed, God's way of salvation through Jesus' death on the cross and resurrection is God's once and for all solution to the sin problem that affected humanity in the fall. Ever since sin entered into the world, God has been on a mission to reconcile humanity back to Himself.

In Jesus Christ, God did for us what we could have never done for ourselves because, of course, Jesus paid the ultimate price to redeem us from our sins. Salvation is a precious gift from God that cost Jesus much suffering, pain and. eventually death; it came, therefore, at the ultimate price.

From a human perspective then, one would think that something so precious would cost something in order to get it. In our consumer-driven society of today, anything that is valuable has a price tag attached to it, and that is usually a monetary price tag. But God does not operate according to the world's system of commerce, transactions and capitalism. God is never motivated by greed or the desire to acquire more wealth. God owns everything already anyway! God is motivated by His love for us and all of creation, so He gives us salvation freely and invites us to accept it by faith, a point we examined in the previous chapter. To try to attach some dollar amount to the value of salvation would be absurd; salvation is truly priceless. The good news of the Gospel is that, in Jesus Christ, salvation is free to ALL and available to ALL. We see this in the bible's use of the word "whosoever" in relation to salvation; the bible and all who read and believe it are destined for salvation. Additionally, we note the following;

1) God is not discriminatory with Salvation.

God's salvation is for all people. He does not allow many of the human issues that divide us from one another dictate whether or not He will save someone. Racism, sexism, ageism, etc… and all of the other "isms" that are so prevalent in our society do not deter God from loving or saving anyone.

2) If people are not saved, it's because they reject God voluntarily.

Since God made us with free will and a mind to make choices, it is possible to reject God's gospel even though it hurts the heart of God. Just like sin is a choice, love must also be a choice. God loved us so much that He gave us free will so that we can voluntarily choose to love Him and serve Him. With that free will, God knows that there is the possibility of rejection as well, but the risk is worth it to God because God is motivated by love. If we were forced to accept the Gospel, it wouldn't be true love or obedience.

3) God can even save "the worst sinner on earth".

While we should not judge others, we must also remember that God's salvation through Jesus Christ can even save those whom we may consider to be the "*worst sinners*"! There is nobody that God cannot save or does not want to save. Even those we think don't deserve it! Paul was a perfect example of this, as he confessed himself in his writing. He acknowledged that he was "chief " among sinners in his past, but God's salvation through Jesus Christ saved him, thereby making him a new person.

Article VII. REGENERATION
Psalm 51:10-12; Psalm 119:10-16; Jeremiah 24:6-7; Ezekiel 11:17-20; John 3:1-8; Romans 12:1-2; 2 Corinthians 5:17-21

Regeneration:

The traditional interpretation of the Articles of Faith:

We believe that the Scriptures teach that in order to be saved, sinners must be regenerated, or born again; that regeneration consists in giving a holy disposition to mind that it is effected in a manner above our comprehension by the power of the Holy Spirit in connection with divine truth, so as to secure our voluntary obedience to the Gospel; and that its proper evidence appears in the holy fruits of repentance and faith, and newness of life.

REMIXED:

We believe that when we experience salvation through Jesus Christ that we are regenerated or "born again". When we truly experience salvation, our nature, our character, our will, and our actions will be changed to be in agreement with the will of God for our lives, and it will also be our desire to grow in this way. Because we have been changed by God, we will change the way we live from now on so that God will be pleased with us.

What does it really mean when we say in the church that we have been "born again"? While it is clear that it is a term that Jesus used in His dialogue with Nicodemus, it is still often misunderstood within both the church and the world.

The world has had a tendency to make fun of Christians who profess to be "born again believers", but as we see from this article of faith, experiencing regeneration is a necessary part of experiencing true salvation. It is not an insincere attempt to become religious in response to tragedy or fear. Regeneration refers to the process by which we are born again, and it is the work of God in us and on us through the Holy Spirit – sincerely and purely.

To be born again means that we have been "converted", "changed", "transformed" or "made new" by God. The point here is that when God saves us, we cannot and should not be the same person with the same nature, same thoughts, same motivations and same actions as we were before God intervenes in our lives. When we are born again, God gives us a renewed heart and mind that in turn give us new actions, thoughts and deeds. When God saves us, He does not simply leave us in the same fallen sinful state that we are in before we meet God. Rather, God re-creates us in His image in order to repair the damage that was done to us by sin. This re-creation by God is not simply on the outside, it is an inner transformation that starts in the heart and the mind and then manifests itself in visible ways on the outside of us.

When you are truly born again, sin and unrighteousness will always bother you. When you are born again, there are certain things that you won't do and won't want to do because they are against God's new nature that He has created in your life. When you are born again, you WANT to do what God wants you to do because your nature now desires to please God. If we are born again, we should truly show signs in our lives that God has indeed changed us. We will act differently, talk differently and treat people differently all because God has changed us. We should proudly and boldly tell the world that we are born again in both our words and deeds! God accomplishes this work in our lives through the Holy Spirit in three basic steps:

1) We are convicted of our sins

One of the functions of the Holy Spirit is to convict us of sin; that is to make us see our sins for what they are and acknowledge that we are guilty. In order to experience true conversion, we must acknowledge what is wrong with the current sinful state that we are in. You can't be transformed from something in your life if you don't feel that there is anything wrong with it and that there is no need to change. As painful as it is sometimes, the Holy Spirit convicts our hearts and minds in order to point out what needs to be changed in us.

2) We repent of our sins

To repent means that we are sorrowful about the sin that God has pointed out in our lives and that we make the willful decision to change from that way of living. Repentance means not only that we regret our sins, but that we decide to change our mind, heart and attitude about them. Even though we don't have all the willpower within us to change ourselves, it is important that we come to the realization that we want to change because the sin that God has exposed to us is painful for us as well as God. We decide we don't want to live this way anymore. The Holy Spirit's intent is to make us face our sin so plainly that we will be moved to sorrow in our heart and a decision and desire to change from it.

3) We confess faith in Jesus Christ

We don't have the ability or the authority to totally re-create ourselves, but Jesus does! The good news of the Gospel is that when we come face to face with our sins and repent of them, that God has provided the means for us to be born again and converted. That way is Jesus Christ and His sacrificial death on the cross and His resurrection from the dead. The Holy Spirit is constantly pointing us and guiding us toward Jesus Christ. When we embrace Jesus as our Lord and Savior by faith, we receive the blessing of being born again, re-created spiritually in the image of God and accepted into the family of God as His child. So the Bible talks about how we are "*new creations*" and how God has made us into transformed people of God. We are born again, saved, converted, changed and transformed. God gives us a new mind, a new heart and a new life. It is now our responsibility to live the life that we have been converted into.

Reader's Remix:
Real-life Reflections on Chapter Three

Salvation and regeneration are not new concepts to us. In fact, as we established earlier, we know what it is to be saved from something – even ourselves, and we know the general meaning of "born again" or regenerated. It is also easy to understand the premise presented to us in this chapter – that God allows us to be born again. It is OK to say that you have been "saved" and know true salvation. Are these passive occurrences, however? Do we wait to be "saved" – do we wait for God to find us and "regenerate" us and our beliefs?

Have I allowed God into my life, and do I live my life

in His example? It is really as simple as that.

As is usually the case with something so precious like these gifts from God – salvation and regeneration, we need to be somewhat active in our own education, and, yes, our own recovery. After all, we did establish that you DO have to admit fault or problems in order to greet God and his plan for your salvation. You do need to be open to being "reborn", "born again", or regenerated – whatever the popular phrase is these days. And, yes, we discussed how people may scoff – laugh even – that you feel you have been reborn. But... as all true believers know – it is the truth. It can be a new way of life, and all those familiar with the Articles of Faith can attest to that.

Understanding the "freeness" of Salvation and accepting Regeneration are, again, big steps in the life of a Christian. We hear these words – salvation – regeneration - during church service on Sunday, but do we really think about WHAT they mean to us as active people in our families, communities, and the world. We hear that God is loving and accepting and extends to us invitations to this life of redemption and acceptance, but... do we really believe that as a fact – a fact as real as the homes we share with our families or as real as the church building in which we worship?

Understanding the "freeness" of Salvation and accepting Regeneration are, again, big steps in the life of a Christian.

This fact remains, to most theologians and religious educators, as plain as the smiles on our faces – yet, to lay people, it isn't always as apparent. We can simply choose to accept God's invitation to Salvation and live life as saved Christians. We can do that. Whether or not we actually take that simple step is another matter entirely.

Ask yourselves – on your way to coffee in the morning – as you work out at the gym – when you take your family on vacation – have I done everything that I can, as a parent, sister, brother, friend – to make my life full and complete? Have I allowed God into my life, and do I live my life in His example? It is really as simple as that.

Chapter 4

Moving on to Repentance and Faith, God's Purpose of Grace, and True Sanctification

Article VIII. REPENTANCE AND FAITH

Ezekiel 14:6, Ezekiel 18:27-32, Matthew 3:1-2, Mark 1:14-15, Luke 15:7; Luke 24:45-49, Acts 2:37-42, 2 Corinthians 7:10, 2 Peter 3:8-9, 1 John 1:8-10

Repentance and Faith:

The traditional interpretation of the Articles of Faith:

We believe the Scriptures teach that repentance and faith are sacred duties, and also inseparable graces, wrought in our souls by the regenerating Spirits of God; whereby being deeply convinced of our guilt, danger and helplessness and of the way of salvation by Christ, we turn to God with unfeigned contrition, confession, and supplication for mercy; at the same time heartily receiving the Lord Jesus Christ as our prophet, priest and king, and relying on him alone as the only and all-sufficient Saviour.

REMIXED:

We believe that repentance and faith are essential for a Christian to truly live according to God's will. Repentance means that we acknowledge that we are sorry for the sins that we have committed against God, and that we are making an intentional choice to not repeat them, but to change the way we live. We are only able to do this because of our faith in Jesus Christ who empowers us and teaches us how to live for God.

This doctrinal teaching shows us that when we are born-again or regenerated, part of the results that become apparent in our lives is that we are moved to repentance and faith. Repentance means literally to turn away from our sins because we are sorrowful that we have rebelled against God. Faith is our belief and trust in God and God's word. As stated in this article, repentance and faith are not only *sacred*, because the Holy Spirit works to bring them alive in our hearts and souls, but repentance and faith are also *inseparable*. That is, when a person is truly born-again, repentance and faith will be hand in hand and a true believer will exhibit evidence of both in his or her life.

> *That is, when a person is truly born-again, repentance and faith will be hand-in-hand and a true believer will exhibit evidence of both in his or her life.*

The reason this doctrinal truth is important to emphasize is because there are those in the world who would be attracted to Jesus as a miracle-worker, but yet don't want to deal with the guilt that comes with confessing their sins and making the decision to turn from these sins. So, people will believe that God through Jesus Christ can bless them, sustain them, heal them, guide them, provide for them, etc…, but not everyone wants to admit to his or her sins, confess them and then turn from them. It is as if some want the "goodies" and benefits that Jesus can give them through faith, but they don't want to repent and deal with the sin that disrupts their relationship with Jesus. That mindset has caused the world to develop a warped understanding of God that has been referred to as "cheap grace". It is as if the sacrifice that Jesus made through His death burial and resurrection is an option that a person may take or leave. But, in the meantime, they want all of the benefits that can come from faith.

If we want God to truly bless us, then it begins with our own souls being converted by God. That conversion begins with repenting from our sins and then continues by accepting the invitation of God to receive salvation through Jesus Christ by faith. The two are inseparable! God's plan of salvation is primarily concerned with our souls and then the blessings move outward to work on our life circumstances as well. The faith that enables us to believe that God is a healer, liberator, provider, guider, etc…is the same faith that also causes us to turn to Jesus Christ as our Savior because we are sorry for the sins that we have committed and confessed. The church of Jesus Christ has to be careful to not proclaim a *lopsided* gospel - that is, a message that ignores the reality of sin and salvation while only telling people about what's in it for them. Some ways we can do this are:

1) **When we testify, tell what God has delivered us from, not just what He gave us**

2) **Be humble enough to repent when we are wrong, even when it may be known by others**

3) **Emphasize a *relationship* with Jesus Christ as Savior and Lord when we witness**

Article IX. GOD'S PURPOSE OF GRACE
Romans 8:26-34, 1 Peter 2:1-10, Ephesians 1:3-14

God's Purpose of Grace:

The traditional interpretation of the Articles of Faith:

We believe the Scriptures teach that election is the eternal purpose of God, according to which he graciously regenerates, sanctifies and saves sinners; that being perfectly consistent with the free agency of man, it comprehends all the means in connection with the end; that it is a most glorious display of God's sovereign goodness, being infinitely free, wise, holy and unchangeable; that it utterly excludes boasting and promotes humility, love, prayer, praise, trust in God, and active imitation of his free mercy; that it encourages the use of means in the highest degree; that it may be ascertained by its effects in all who truly believe the Gospel; that it is the foundation of Christian assurance; and that to ascertain it with regard to ourselves demands and deserves the utmost diligence.

REMIXED:

We believe that Christians, who are in Christ, are considered to be chosen, predestined, or part of the elect by God, because Jesus Christ has given our life new meaning, new purpose and a new destination. We are only in Christ by the grace of God, and therefore all of the new possibilities and purposes that come into our lives because of our relationship with Jesus Christ are gifts from God. God's purpose of grace is to bring us back into a right relationship with Him as it existed before sin affected humanity; it is God working on our behalf and bringing us into His will for us. It is a precious gift that we could never earn for ourselves.

The words *"chosen"*, *"predestination"* and *"elect"* are words that have been a source of much misunderstanding and debate in the Christian church for centuries. All of these words, on the surface, imply that human beings have a predetermined destiny or future that will definitely be fulfilled regardless of what they may say or do or how they may live. In our society, we say, many times, that something is "fate", "karma", "destiny" or that something is "just meant to be". Whatever the case, we have to be careful about applying a "whatever will be, will be" mentality to our lives indiscriminately, especially when it comes to our faith.

This doctrinal teaching of the church challenges us to think about God's eternal redemptive purpose for all of humanity and creation as well as how that purpose is founded upon love and made possible by grace. When we say "grace", we are referring to God's unmerited favor that He bestows upon us. There is nothing that we do to earn favor from the heart of God; instead, God chooses to love us, save us and redeem us out of God's own heart and character. God chose to send Jesus Christ. Jesus Christ chose to die on the cross. God chose to put the plan of salvation into action for us. God chose us, and as the bible teaches us it is our choice to love God back and to choose to live for Him.

Unfortunately, throughout world history this doctrine has been misused, misapplied and abused by groups of people who have claimed to be God's "chosen people" and have, therefore, used it to justify their own opinions and actions that are inconsistent with the nature and character of God. Hate groups, terrorist groups and politically and socially oppressive groups and even nations have been and still do use God's name and purpose to justify ungodly stances and actions in the world because they believe they have been "chosen" by God to do so.

But this doctrinal teaching exposes the faulty nature of all of them by telling us that God extends love, grace and salvation to ALL people without prejudice or exclusion; and that ALL people have the free will to accept or reject God's invitation to salvation. Our choices as human beings do matter, and they do have consequences. God has created this world, and He has created us so that our choices in life can create all different types of consequences and, ultimately, change our future and destiny. God is a God of love, and humanity is created to be morally responsible and accountable. The issues of election, predestination, and being chosen must properly be understood in the biblical context of being *"in Christ"*. When it comes to this article of faith, we must remember the following:

1) God is sovereign, and has self-imposed limitations

We know and believe that God is all-powerful and can do anything that God wants to. But God also is faithful and keeps His word, so God will not act contrary to His word, His purpose or His nature. God does not have to ask anyone's permission to act, but He always acts in accordance with His own laws and nature. God always works within the boundaries of love and righteousness, which God Himself created. So, since God created us with a free will, He would never impose or force us to love Him or anyone else. It is a choice that we must make. God has the power to force us or make us to love Himself and everyone else, but that would be contrary to God's nature and His word. His grace comes to us in the form of an invitation, and even though He has the power to force it on us, God would not do that because it is contrary to His promise.

2) Humanity has a free will that makes us morally responsible and accountable

God created us with the ability to choose; therefore, we are responsible for our choices and the consequences that come from them. We cannot make choices and then blame God for the results, especially if we choose to do something that is outside of God's biblical standards of righteousness. Likewise, if things go well in our lives, we should not steal the credit for it as if God has not blessed us. God gave us free will so that we can respond willingly to God's invitation to be in a loving, saving relationship with Him. If we reject God, there are consequences that we must face. It is not God's desire for anyone to perish, but God knows that if we have free will, then some may choose to reject Him. God does not play favorites with people in creation. While some may have a different purpose, position or place in life; God's overall desire remains consistent throughout time. God wants all people to be saved and blessed and invites us to be with Him.

3) We are "elect", "chosen" and "predestined" in Christ

The key to understanding what being chosen really means

lies in understanding what it means to be in a relationship with God through Jesus Christ. Notice how many times the bible talks about being "in Christ" or its equivalent in Ephesians 1. When we are "in Christ", it is then that we are blessed to be included with those who have a predetermined destiny, who are chosen as a peculiar (or special) people and are a part of God's elect body of believers who are in fellowship with Him. Being "in Christ" is what determines our destiny and gives us assurance and confidence that we are safely and securely in the hands of God. Our purpose and our future are already set and defined because we are "in Christ". Not limited to the earthly, temporary existence in this world, being "in Christ" gives us

an eternal destiny that far surpasses anything that this world may offer. God's love causes God to extend His grace to us in the form of an invitation to new life and relationship with Him. When we use our free will to choose Jesus Christ, then we are blessed to be born into the body of Christ, the elect, the chosen, the predestined from the foundation of the world.

Article X. SANCTIFICATION
John 17:15-21, Romans 15:16, 1 Corinthians 1:2 & 6:9-11
Ephesians 5:24-29, 2 Timothy 2:19-21, 1 Thess. 4:1-7,
Hebrews 10:10 & 13:12

Sanctification:

The traditional interpretation of the Articles of Faith: We believe the Scriptures teach that Sanctification is the process by which, according to will of God, we are made partakers of His holiness; that it is a progressive work; that it is begun in regeneration; and that it is carried on in the hearts of believers by the presence and power of the Holy Spirit, the Sealer and Comforter, in the continual use of the appointed means especially the word of God, self-examination, self-denial, watchfulness and prayer.

REMIXED:

We believe that once we experience salvation, God begins a process in our hearts called sanctification that is intended to make us holy, just as God is holy. Although salvation is instantaneous; sanctification is a process by which God makes us holy inwardly in our hearts and outwardly in our actions. God accomplishes this process in us through the presence and power of the Holy Spirit, by teaching us in the bible, and by communicating with us through our prayer lives.

The word "sanctification" is one that has been, unfortunately, misunderstood and misused by many within the church of today. It seems that, somehow, this word has been labeled or categorized as a description that is often applied to some churches that have a more charismatic style of worship. For years, I have heard people talk about "sanctified churches" as if they are somehow a different denomination among themselves. Likewise, there was also a phrase that people used when they testified, which was that they were "saved, sanctified and filled with the Holy Ghost." This terminology was also labeled and characterized to be referring to a sanctified group of people who were like a separate group of Christians with a different style of worship and with different rules for living their daily lives.

This article of faith teaches us that ALL churches should be sanctified churches, and ALL true Christians are indeed sanctified. To be "sanctified" does not simply refer to a particular characterization or style. Sanctification is the process by which God makes us holy. To be holy means to be set apart and totally committed to God's purpose and will for our lives both individually and collectively as a church. Sanctification is a part of the activity that God wants to accomplish in us as a result of our salvation. While salvation is instantaneous, sanctification is the process by which God progressively makes us just like Himself; Holy. As with the other doctrinal teachings, this is only accomplished through our relationship with God through Jesus Christ. That is, we cannot sanctify ourselves, it is the work of God that is made possible through Jesus Christ and is carried out by the presence of the Holy Spirit in the heart of believers.

We are all sanctified and should not be ashamed or embarrassed to be described as sanctified. The world and our culture have made fun of this concept as if it is irrelevant or a "holier than though" attitude. But in reality, being sanctified is an admission and confession that we understand that God is still working on us to make us holy, like Himself. God proclaims that we are sanctified, and then God continues to work in our lives to bring us into that reality. God constantly shows us how to make better choices in our daily lives – how to speak better and develop better habits, in general, for example. We learn to apply these things to our own lives by getting closer to God ourselves and by watching other Christians who are good examples in the same way. Sanctification gives us new ways of acting, thinking, and being. All of it - our unholy ways, our apathy and more - does not change overnight because we still wrestle with the sinfulness of our flesh, but, spiritually, God is constantly converting us and transforming us into the new creations about which the Bible talks.

Regarding sanctification it is important to remember the following:

1) Sanctification is a continual, progressive process of God's work in us.

It is interesting to note how the Bible calls the church in Corinth "sanctified" and "saints" and then goes on to describe their sins and ungodly actions! This lets us know that, while God pronounces our new identity, we are not yet all that we are supposed to be. God continues to work on us and in us in the midst of our moral and spiritual failures and imperfections. When we get saved, we are not perfect right away! But God does have an expectation that we improve and become more like Him as time goes by. The longer we walk with God, the more like Him we should be! We can see then how it must truly grieve the heart of God when we resist His will for us and continually rebel against Him when we truly know better. God is in the process of trying to work in our lives for our good and make us more like Him, and when we sin, we rebel and reject Him. The Christian life is one of self-denial in which we must constantly learn to say no to self and yes to God; the only way that we will be able to be obedient like that is if we mature and grow in our relationship to

God. It should be the desire of every Christian to be more and more like Jesus every day. We ought to be able to look back over our lives and see how we are MORE like Jesus today than we were yesterday, last week, last month, or last year.

2) Sanctification comes as we embrace the truth of God's word.

The Bible, God's word is the blueprint and guide that shows us how to live like God wants us to live. The word of God sanctifies us because it is a light that guides us in the way that God wants us to go. If the Bible tells us to do something, we can trust that doing it will help us to grow to be more like God. If the Bible tells us not to do something, then we can trust that doing it is working against the process of becoming more like Jesus. The more we get into the word of God, and let the word of God get into us; the more we are able to act, think and be like God wants us to be. If we don't know God's word, we can't be fully sanctified properly the way God created us to be because we will inevitably break various parts of the blueprint that God has given us. That's why it is possible for people to be in the church, but not be like Jesus! Our culture nowadays, even in the church is largely biblically illiterate. When we don't know God's word and follow our own blueprint, we end up becoming who WE want to be instead of who God wants us to be. Faith comes by hearing the word of God and embracing its truth. When we do that, then the Holy Spirit has a strong foundation from which to work in our hearts and minds.

3) The Holy Spirit sanctifies us in our hearts and minds.

The Holy Spirit is God, and what a blessing that God lives in us! Every day, as we live in the presence of God we are being molded and shaped because of the presence of the Holy Spirit within us. We are not 100% transformed and converted in an instant, but the presence of the Holy Spirit does His perfect work in our lives and progressively breaks down sinful strongholds that are robbing us of the fullness of God's image in us. Everyday, the presence of the Holy Spirit regulates our minds and guides our hearts and actions. The Holy Spirit convicts us of our sins, brings things to our remembrance, moves us to take Godly actions, tells us when to sit still and wait, and even helps us love and forgive one another. The Holy Spirit even prays for us when we don't know what to pray for! All of this activity and more is a part of God sanctifying us and making us Holy. It is God's will for us to be sanctified until we are just like Him.

Reader's Remix:
Real-life Reflections on Chapter Four

Again, it is up to us to make sure that we truly receive repentance and faith – and God's grace – and sanctification.... all that makes us faithful Christians. Yes, we know God, and we know what we need to do, in most cases, to be better people, but do we always completely understand what it takes to allow the Holy Spirit to guide our lives – to allow God into our lives with an almost blind faith – to live in the image of Jesus Christ and all that can be accomplished for the world? What does all this mean?

It is often easy to say that we have been "saved" – that we have truly "repented" and know what it takes to get others to do the same. And, sure, maybe we have been sorry for what we've done, changed our ways, and gone forth to show others, by example, how to live. But... do we allow new opportunities for faith and love and understanding into our lives? Do we listen to the sermon at church – maybe even read the Bible – but never reach out to our fellow man or apply what we hear, what we read, and what we absorb to our daily lives? It is time to do this. It is time to be the Christians that God intended us to be – not some imitation of what we think we see, hear, and read.

Can we really, truly practice self-denial to the degree that we try to live as God wanted us to – before sin affected our lives? And, can we carry with us, in our hearts, this complete sense of good will and inherent Christianity wherever we go? I think we can. In fact, I think it is possible to reach out daily – to those who may not have accepted Jesus into their lives – who may not even know how to live as God wants us to. How difficult is it to spread His message - to tell others of the Glory of God and our roles in it? Not difficult at all for the seasoned and educated Christian – one who has a full understanding of our Articles of Faith.

Chapter 5

The Saints, the Law, the Gospel, and a Gospel Church

Article XI. PERSEVERANCE OF SAINTS

John 10:27-29, 1 Corinthians 6:20, Ephesians 1:12-14, 2 Timothy 1:8-14

The traditional interpretation of the Articles of Faith:

We believe the Scriptures teach that such only are real believers as endure to the end; that their persevering attachment of Christ is the grand mark which distinguishes them from superficial professors; that a special Providence watches over their welfare; and they are kept by the power of God through faith unto salvation.

REMIXED:

We believe that when we experience truly authentic salvation from God through Jesus Christ, that it is a reality that endures and lasts not just until the end of our lives, but until the end of time when Jesus comes back to judge the world. Real saints who have truly been born again endure to the end, and cannot and do not lose their salvation because it is a gift from God and it is in God's hands. While there may be those who are falsely professing to know Jesus, whose religion will not endure; the true saints of God are securely kept by the grace of God and sealed until the day of redemption by the Holy Spirit.

The doctrine that is expressed in this article of faith is important because it teaches that God's work of Salvation, Regeneration and Sanctification are not just simply one-time temporary activities in our lives that don't last. When we are truly born- again and saved by God through Jesus Christ, that activity of God is real, and we are transformed in ways that will change us forever. Real Christians go all the way with God and endure until the end. In one sense, "the end" means until the end of our lives, but, in a more profound sense, it also means until Jesus comes back to judge the world in the end times of all creation.

Real Christians who have truly experienced the saving power of God through Jesus Christ in their lives are not just like a "flash in the pan" who might be here with God today then gone tomorrow. Real Christians or "saints" go all the way with God in their lives and persevere until the end; we remain faithful and committed to God until the end of our lives and beyond into eternal life. We don't quit on God because we don't want to quit on God. When we think about the goodness of God and what He has saved us from and how He has given us new life, we are moved and motivated to stay with God until the end, no matter what. That does not mean that we sometimes don't struggle or even fall into temptation to sin in life, but we never quit God because our salvation is in *HIS* hands and not ours! In fact *we* are even in His hands, not our own. So since salvation is the work of God and not us, the same God who saved us is able to keep us, preserve us and guarantee us until the final day of redemption. In other words, when you are truly saved by God, you don't lose your salvation or somehow turn your back on it. Even when we sin or stray, the promises and provisions of God are still in effect; we can still confess our sins, repent, and be forgiven by God.

Over the years there have been many debates about whether or not people could lose their salvation or intentionally turn away from it. The scriptures teach that this concept is not true, and in the cases where it appears to have happened, the original salvation experience was not truly sincere and authentic. For example, Judas Iscariot, who was one of the 12 apostles in the New Testament, is the case that is often cited because he eventually turned away from Jesus and betrayed Him. However, as this doctrinal teaching reveals, he was a spiritual pretender, a disciple who acts like he knows Jesus and has been saved by Him, but in reality, none of this holds true. Although this is not a common occurrence, there is evidence to suggest that it does happen throughout both the Old and New Testament.

Unfortunately, even in the church, there are people who may profess to know Jesus Christ who really don't. There is a distinct difference between knowing Jesus Christ as your personal Lord and Savior and knowing *about* Jesus Christ as a great teacher, preacher, leader or philosopher. People may sound the same, look the same and even go to church the same, but inwardly, Jesus Christ is not truly Lord and Savior to some. Others do accept Him as their only savior – the greatest teacher in their lives. Only God truly knows who is who, and only God is the rightful judge. The truth will come out in the end on Judgment Day, because a superficial, surface relationship with Jesus Christ will not persevere until the end like authentic salvation will. God knows the true believers; God knows the heart of people, ultimately. So, as a result, that's why people can come and join churches and profess to Jesus Christ, but then never come back or be seen in the church again. These people did not profess a faith in Jesus Christ or commit to Him in a way that would truly persevere. On the other side, there are also those who are like the prodigal son (Luke: Chapter 15) who are with God and then take an unfortunate detour away from God but eventually end up understanding themselves – their shortcomings and strengths - and coming back to God with a greater appreciation. However the process happens, real Christians don't quit or disappear on God for good because:

1) Jesus holds us in His hands.

Jesus said Himself that God the Father gave us to Him, and that nobody can ever take us out of His hand. We are His sheep and we know His voice. When we experience real salvation, Jesus Himself holds us in His hands for our protection, guidance and safekeeping. It is a comfort to know that through all of the many experiences that may happen to us in life, both positive and negative, that Jesus is always holding us in His hands. He takes care of us and nothing happens to us that is not subject to the authority of His hands. His hand represents power, and that power is what helps us to persevere. Not our will power, but His power! Rely on His power, not your own. God will keep you!

2) The Holy Spirit seals us.

Not only does Jesus hold us in His hands, but the Holy Spirit is the seal or guarantee that further keeps us safe and secure until the day of redemption. The presence and the power of the Holy Spirit in our lives is God's divine seal that guarantees the validity and authenticity of God's salvation in our lives. The Holy Spirit is the sign of God's promise to us to never leave us or forsake us. When God places the Holy Spirit in our lives, it is like His personal guarantee that He will keep His word to us and do everything that He has promised to do for us. So we are comforted by the presence of the Holy Spirit in our lives because every time we see a manifestation of the Holy Spirit, we are reminded that God will keep His promises and that He is going to complete the work of salvation, regeneration and sanctification that He has started in our lives.

God perseveres for us; let us also persevere with Him!

3) We know that we belong to God.

The love of Jesus Christ and the presence and power of the Holy Spirit are constant reminders to every child of God that we do *belong* to God. We are His people, His workmanship, His children and the objects of His love. Now that we know that we belong to God, we should live like we belong to Him instead of the many worldly influences that also seek to own us improperly. Jesus Christ is the only one who has saved us and redeemed us, so why then should I live as if I am the property of someone or something else in the world? We are moved and motivated to persevere and to stay with God because ultimately God is the only one that has expressed how valuable we are by sending Jesus Christ to die for our sins. So, since we belong to Him, let's live for Him and stay with Him. Other worldly powers and people may claim us temporarily, but when our usefulness runs out, they will abandon us. God through Jesus Christ is the only one who has literally given His life for us.

He has committed Himself to saving us and loving us until the end. God perseveres for us; let us also persevere with Him!

Article XII. THE LAW AND GOSPEL

Exodus 20:1-17, Matthew 5:17-26, Romans 7:4-14, Galatians 2:16-21 & 3:24-26

The traditional interpretation of the Articles of Faith:

We believe the Scriptures teach that the Law of God is the eternal and unchangeable rule of his moral government; that it is holy, just and good; and that the inability which the Scriptures ascribe to fallen men to fulfill its precepts, arise entirely from their love of sin; to deliver them from which, and to restore them through a Mediator to unfeigned obedience to the holy Law, is one great end of the Gospel, and of the Means of Grace connected with the establishment of the visible church.

REMIXED:

We believe that the laws of God as revealed in the bible are holy, just and good; and that human beings are incapable of fully obeying God's laws on our own. We need the blessings of the Gospel of Jesus Christ to help us to fulfill God's laws. In essence, the law of God points out our need for the Gospel in our lives because it exposes our sins. What we cannot do through human effort, Jesus Christ does for us in the Gospel story; therefore, law and Gospel go hand in hand for Christians.

This article highlights an important doctrinal teaching that helps us to bring balance to our understanding regarding why we need the Gospel of Jesus Christ. In it, we see that the Law of God is holy, just, and good. That is certainly true since the Law reveals God's expectations of us as human beings and His standards for holiness and righteousness in our daily living as we worship God and interact with each other. When we talk about the "Law", we must make some important biblical distinctions. Traditionally, when we see the word "law" in the New Testament, we think of it as referring to the 10 Commandments, otherwise known as the *Decalogue*. But the "law" also encompasses more than that! The Mosaic Law consists not only of the Decalogue in Exodus 20-23; but also the *Deuteronomic code* and the book of the law that are found in the book of Deuteronomy. The word *Deuteronomy* literally means *second law* and it is traditionally understood that God was re-stating His laws a second time for Israel before they entered into the Promised Land. The Mosaic Law also includes what is known as the *Holiness Code*, which appears in Leviticus chapters 17-26 where we see many straightforward dos and don'ts from God related to what is holy and proper and what is not. In all, the Mosaic Law is thought to consist of well over 600 laws and commandments that God told Israel to keep!

When we think about this in light of what Jesus says to us in the New Testament about the law, the reasons for thanking God for salvation through Jesus Christ become even more apparent. What human being could possibly keep all of the law of God perfectly without messing up? The answer is no one! Even when the Israelites did sin and would go through the ritual of sacrificing an animal for their sins; that soon became just another empty, meaningless ritual or practice that people did with their heads but not their hearts. They simply went through the motions to try to appease themselves and God.

But God loves us and is always interested in our souls and our salvation. What we could not do through human effort, Jesus Christ did! He was the only human being without sin! That's what enabled Him to be the perfect sacrifice for the sins of the whole world! The Fall of Man caused us to be blemished by sin and incapable of fulfilling God's standards of holiness and righteousness that He has for us. So, God did it for us in Jesus Christ! The Law is good and holy because it seeks to guide us into being who God wants us to be, but it also at the same time condemns us because of our inability to keep it consistently. That is what points us toward the Gospel of Jesus Christ as the only solution to our dilemma. Jesus fulfills the law for us, and when we accept Jesus Christ as our savior by faith, we inherit the salvation that His sacrifice makes possible for us. Although we did not obey the law, since Jesus did and we are in Him, we inherit His righteousness by faith and we must now live up to it. The law brought us to the point of seeing where we are incapable of being consistently obedient to God's law on our own, and therefore enabled us to see the need for Jesus Christ.

Regarding these issues of the Law and the Gospel, it is important for us to note the following:

Breaking the Law is an act of rebellion against God

Whenever we do not live up to the standards of holiness and righteousness that God intended for us when He created us, it is sin. The laws are not simply polite recommendations from God about how we should live; they are God's blueprint for how we should live. When we break them, we break God's plan and purpose for our lives. The irony is that sin tries to use the law to tempt us and condemn us when God's intent is to use the law to bless us.

The purpose of the Law is to bring us into total submission to God

Obedience is important to God. God's law is designed to bring us to a point where we are truly in His image. Total obedience and total submission is what God expects from us since He is sovereign over us. It is clear that what the law could not do for us, Jesus Christ and the Holy Spirit can! The law is able to point the way and express the demands of God, but it cannot save us from the penalties of disobedience. Only Jesus can do that, and only the Holy Spirit can sanctify us and help us to live holy. Jesus is the fulfillment of the Law completely! Now we can and should submit to God in *every* area of our lives.

The Law is a Community responsibility

Church families and communities have a responsibility to follow God's law in our interactions with each other. God is concerned with the holiness of not just individuals, but also homes, families, churches, communities and nations. We are responsible to one another and we must live righteously with one another.

The Law is an individual responsibility

Each person is also responsible for making a faith commitment to God through Jesus Christ and deciding to live God's way. In order for families, churches, communities and nations to change, it begins with individuals. Every child of God must decide that he/she wants to be holy and live holy for God.

Article XIII. A GOSPEL CHURCH
Matthew 16:18, 18:17; Colossians 1:16-18; Acts 2:47, 12:1, 20:28-30; 1 Corinthians 12:27-31; Ephesians 3:20-21, 5:23-32; 1 Timothy 3:1-16

The traditional interpretation of the Articles of Faith:
We believe the Scriptures teach that a visible church of Christ is a congregation of baptized believers, associated by covenant in the faith and fellowship of the Gospel; observing the ordinances of Christ; governed by his laws; and exercising the gifts, rights, and privileges invested in them by His Word; that its only scriptural officers are Bishops or Pastors, and Deacons whose Qualifications, claims and duties are defined in the Epistles to Timothy and Titus.

REMIXED:
We believe that God established the church as the body of Christ for the mutual edification and nurturing of Christians, and that it consists of baptized believers who are in relationship with God and one another; and are called by God to carry the Gospel into the world in both word and deed. The church belongs to God, and it is governed by the Holy Bible in all matters and methods. The only official servant-leaders of the church are the Pastors or Bishops, and

the Deacons; whose duties, qualifications and functions are described in the bible.

This doctrinal teaching introduces us to the concept that the **church** is an intentional part of God's will for the spiritual growth and development of Christians, as well as for the spread of the Gospel throughout the whole world. The church is referred to by several other names in the bible such as; *"flock"*, *"congregation"*, *"assembly"*, *"the way"*, and *"body of Christ"*. All of these names refer to the church that God established, and where Jesus Christ is the head.

The word *"church"* as it appears in the bible literally translates from the Greek word as *"the called-out assembly of people"*. So, it is an important distinction to understand that when the bible talks about the church as God intended it, it does not refer to a building or a business as we sometimes categorize the church. "**Church**" means an assembly of people who have been called out of a worldly, ungodly way of life into a new life in relationship with God through Jesus Christ. A church is a congregation of people who have been baptized as believers in Jesus Christ and choose to freely associate with each other in a covenant relationship based on our faith and a fellowship based on the principles of the Gospel and God's word.

An important point to understand about the church is that as Christians, God desires for us to grow and be nurtured in our faith in the context of meaningful **relationships** with other Christians. Christianity is a religion in which **relationships** are necessary if we are to truly be a Christian. We do not become the Christians that we are supposed to be in isolation away from other people. Although salvation experience is personal, we become more Christ-like as we interact with other people. The institution that God has created and designed to help us grow in our faith with meaningful relationships is the church! So, the church is different than any other organization or institution known to humanity that people may join. The church is not like a fraternity, sorority, non-profit, political party, social agency, club, society, or any other type of organization established by human beings on earth. The church was designed and established by God Himself, and Jesus Christ is the Head. In fact, the church is so special that the bible describes the church as being the "bride" of Christ and the "body" of Christ. No other organization on earth can claim such intimacy with God as the church can.

This is important to understand since we are living in post-modern times when people are beginning to question the relevancy and the need for the church. There are those who embrace the need for religion and spirituality, but resent the organized, institutionalized form of religion that the church represents. However, they fail to realize that the church was founded and established by God! Because of the presence of human beings, the church has its issues and problems to be sure. But the church is still an essential part of God's plan for helping His people become more like Him. Just as God is a God of relationship; Father-Son-Holy Ghost, so must we be people who rely on relationships to be like God. We need each other! God has blessed us with a wonderful fellowship called the church!

As it relates to the church, it is important for us to note the following:

The Meaning of the Church

God means for the church to be the fellowship and place where we live out our faith on a daily basis in relationships with each other and with God. The Church is a place of salvation, nurturing, encouragement, discipline, edification, healing, liberation and spiritual growth. All of these things are in Jesus Christ, and we are the body of Christ in the church. When the world sees the church, they should see Jesus Christ. The church exists as a living testimony in the world that God is real and that Jesus Christ is a living savior. The church is the place on earth where the bible governs all our actions, decisions, thoughts and deeds. In the church, the Kingdom of God and its principles are lived as a reality on earth even though we are surrounded by a world that does not believe in God. In order to do this, we must love each other, encourage each other and strengthen each other; and we do it in the context of the church!

The Message of the Church

The message of the church is the Gospel of Jesus Christ. That God took on the form of humanity in the person of Jesus Christ. That Jesus Christ died on the cross of Calvary, but rose from the dead on Resurrection Day. Our message is that God, through Jesus Christ has provided the way for humanity to have new life and everlasting life. It is a message of hope, healing, salvation, deliverance and love for all who have been beaten up and bruised by life in this ungodly world.

The Make-up of the Church

As stated in the article, the church consists of baptized believers in the Lord Jesus Christ. Among the congregation, there are two Biblical offices that God intended; Pastor (Bishop) and Deacon. These are the only two Biblical offices of the church. The Pastor is also referred to as Bishop, Minister, Elder or Apostle in the Bible. These two offices are the only two that scripture describes as ordained to a particular service. Pastor/Bishop means overseer or one who leads the flock; while Deacon means servant. There are other offices and titles in the church that are man-made, but these two were established scripturally in the early church.

The Mission of the Church

The mission of the church is expressed in Matthew 28:19-20, otherwise known as the Great Commission. We are to carry the message of the Gospel of Jesus Christ into the whole world. We are to teach people and baptize people. We are to tell people about the salvation that is available through Jesus Christ. That is our first, foundational, main message. That message then has implications for us as a church. Because of that message, we minister and serve humanity and their needs, so we feed the hungry, clothe the naked, comfort the bereaved, counsel the lost, advocate for the downtrodden and poor, etc… Our mission is a global mission, so we must understand ourselves as a part of something much bigger than our local church. We are a part of the *Church Universal*, and as such we must do our part in cooperation with all of God's local churches. As a part of the *Church Universal*, we work toward our mission of making the Kingdom of God a living reality here on earth.

Reader's Remix:
Real-life Reflections on Chapter Five

We have established in this chapter that following God and being close members of the church are intrinsically linked. One concept cannot exist without the other; we cannot be good, informed, educated, and devoted Christians who profess Jesus Christ as our one and only savior unless we do attend and become immersed in the teachings of the church. We need to attend services, respect our church leaders, and listen, learn, and apply the teachings of Jesus Christ to our daily lives.

Beyond our physical presence in the church, we need to understand the spiritual implications of being part of such a grand and noble community. God's church is an important guiding force in our lives – married to God in ideology and practice, the church is what should inform our lives in every way. This is something to remember, strive for, and communicate to others. Once implemented in a person's life, it should be talked about in the community. Our goal as church-going Christians should be to act as good examples of faithful people of God who persevere as opposed to those who stray easily from the faith.

Chapter 6

Baptism, the Lord's Supper, and the Christian Sabbath

Article XIV. BAPTISM AND THE LORD'S SUPPER

Matthew 3:16; Matthew 28:19; Acts 2:37-38; Acts 8:36-39; Galatians 3:27; Romans 6:1-6; Matthew 26:26-30; Mark 10:38-39 & 14:22-26; Luke 22:15-20; 1 Corinthians 11:23-30; 1 Corinthians 12:13; Colossians 2:11-12

The traditional interpretation of the Articles of Faith:

We believe the Scriptures teach that Christian baptism is the immersion in water of a believer, into the name of the Father, and Son, and Holy Ghost; to show forth in a solemn and beautiful emblem, our faith in crucified, buried, and risen Saviour, with its effect, in our death to sin and resurrection to a new life; that it is prerequisite to the privileges of a church, by the sacred use of bread and wine, are to commemorate together the dying love of Christ; preceded always by solemn self-examination.

REMIXED:

We believe that baptism is an ordinance that we submit to as an outward sign or witness that we have experienced salvation through Jesus Christ. Baptism is done by immersion of the believer in water in the name of the Father, and of the Son and of the Holy Spirit; it signifies our death to sin and our resurrection to new life in Jesus Christ.

We further believe that the Lord's Supper is an ordinance that we practice in the church that commemorates the death, burial and resurrection of Jesus Christ. The bread signifies the body of our Lord Jesus Christ, which He gave to die on the cross of Calvary; and the cup signifies His blood, which was shed at Calvary for the forgiveness of our sins. Whenever we do it, it is done in remembrance of Jesus Christ.

In this article of Faith, we learn that the two primary ordinances of the church are Baptism and the Lord's Supper, otherwise known as Communion. While different denominations may have different views on whether or not other rituals should be included as an ordinance, most Christian denominations agree on these two as the two basic ordinances. We should note that there is a difference between an *ordinance* and a *sacrament* in the language and conversation of the church. A sacrament is generally believed to be a sacred ritual in the church that is connected with some mystical, supernatural power or actual conveyance of grace. In other words, it is believed that just the act of participating in a sacrament literally does something mystical and supernatural in the life of the person who is involved.

By contrast, an *ordinance* is a symbol, and does not incorporate the idea of conveying grace or mystical and supernatural activity. Since an ordinance is a symbol, it has no inherent power to change those who are participating in it, although God can certainly use the act to minister to a person's heart. We believe that Baptism and Communion are ordinances of the church because the water itself does not save people in Baptism and neither do the bread and wine in Communion. They are simply symbols, and the act of participating in the ordinances symbolizes something profound in God's ministry and presence in the world.

The ordinance of Baptism is a symbolic act whereby a person who professes belief in Jesus Christ submits to being immersed in water as a public profession of their faith and a sign to the world that they are a follower of Jesus Christ. The symbolism of baptism mirrors the death, burial and resurrection of Jesus Christ. Going down under the water symbolizes death and burial to our old way of life in the world, and coming up out of the water symbolizes the resurrection to new life that we have been blessed with by Jesus Christ. While there are other methods of baptism that exist in various other Christian denominations which include sprinkling and pouring water over just the head of the person, the Baptist church practices immersion because it is the way in which Jesus Himself was baptized by John the Baptist in the Jordan river.

Another important distinction in the ordinance of baptism is that we practice what is called *believer's baptism*. That means that we only baptize people who have personally confessed a belief in Jesus Christ for themselves. In many of the biblical stories, what made people ready to be baptized was the moment they made a personal confession of faith in Jesus Christ. For this reason, the Baptist church does not baptize infants. Rather, we bless babies and then covenant together with the parents and God-parents to be examples of Christ and pro- vide the nurturing and teaching to help the baby grow up to, ultimately, one day make his or her own personal confession of faith in Jesus Christ. There is one instance of re-baptism in the Bible which occurs in Acts 19:1-5 that further supports the necessity of belief in Jesus Christ before baptism. In this case, there were several disciples who had only been exposed to the Baptism of Repentance that John the Baptist had administered. When Paul met these disciples, he taught them about Jesus Christ, and they were then baptized in the name of Jesus. In essence, their previous and first baptism was incomplete and uninformed. In order to be baptized properly, they had to know about Jesus Christ beforehand.

Believer's baptism is an important doctrine of the church also because we see in scripture how baptism has other degrees of spiritual meaning in the life of a Christian. Baptism also symbolizes that we are a part of the body of Christ, which is the church. It also signifies that we are participants in Christ's suffering; that we have received God's forgiveness, that we have repented of our sins, and that we have committed ourselves to making disciples for Jesus Christ.

Regarding this ordinance of baptism, it is important to remember:
- Jesus Himself submitted to being baptized and so should we.
- Belief in Jesus Christ is essential before being baptized.
- Baptism is a public profession for us to tell the world that we believe in Jesus Christ.
- Baptism symbolizes the death, burial and resurrection of Jesus Christ.
- Baptism means that we have chosen to fully associate our lives with Jesus Christ and His church.
- Immersion is the chosen method of baptism in the Baptist church.

The Lord's Supper, otherwise known as Communion is an ordinance of the church whereby we remember our Lord Jesus

Christ. We commemorate His death on the cross and the fact that He is coming back again to judge the world. We know from scripture that Jesus Himself instituted the Lord's Supper, which he celebrated with the 12 apostles around the time of the Passover. Jesus took bread and blessed it and broke it and gave it to them and said *"take, eat, this is my body"*. Likewise, Jesus then took the cup and gave it to them and said *"drink ye all of it; for this is my blood of the New Testament, which is shed for many for the remission of sins."* In these acts and with these words, Jesus instituted what we call "The Lord's Supper". When we partake of Communion, we are symbolically participating with and embracing the body and blood of Jesus Christ and all that they mean to the life of a believer. It is no surprise then that Baptism is a pre-requisite before a person may take communion in the Baptist church. Only believers in Jesus Christ can fully participate and commune with Jesus Christ in this way.

The two traditional schools of thought regarding Communion are *transubstantiation and consubstantiation*. For centuries in the Christian church, theologians have argued over these differing viewpoints. In *transubstantiation*, it is believed that the bread and wine literally are transformed into the actual body and blood of Jesus Christ. This view sees communion as more of a sacrament. In *consubstantiation*, it is believed that the presence of Jesus Christ is with us spiritually in the moment when we partake of the body and blood of Christ. Since we see communion as an ordinance, we hold to the doctrine of con- substantiation since the symbolism of the act communicates divine truth to us, but the bread and wine themselves do not have any mystical or supernatural ability to impart grace.

Jesus said as often as we take Communion, we do it in remembrance of Him. So, Communion is an act whereby we remember Jesus Christ, His sacrificial death that He suffered for us, and that He is coming back again. Some churches may do it monthly, weekly, or even annually, but what is important is that it is done in remembrance of Jesus. Another important part of Communion is the self-examination that every Christian should do before partaking. It is a time for us to look at ourselves and see our own faults and failings and ask God's forgiveness. In this way, we are taking Jesus' body and blood seriously and not taking it for granted. Jesus paid it all for us, and all to Him we owe!

It is a time for us to look at ourselves and see our own faults and failings and ask God's forgiveness.

Article XV. THE CHRISTIAN SABBATH
Genesis 2:1-3; Exodus 20:8-11; Isaiah 58:13-14; Matthew 12:1-14; Mark 2:23-28; John 20:1, 19; Acts 20:7; 1 Corinthians 16:2; Revelation 1:10-11

The traditional interpretation of the Articles of Faith:
We believe the Scriptures teach that the first day of the week is the Lord's Day, or Christian Sabbath, and is to be kept sacred to religious purposes, by abstaining from all secular labor and sinful recreations, by the devout observance of all the means of grace, both private and public, and by a preparation for that rest that remaineth for the people of God.

REMIXED:

We believe that the first day of the week, Sunday, is the Christian Sabbath or the Lord's Day. The Christian Sabbath is a holy day because it is the day that Jesus was resurrected from the dead. It has its roots in the Old Testament Sabbath, and should therefore be observed as a day of worship, rest and meditation on our life with God and the church both privately and publicly.

The Christian Sabbath is a doctrinal teaching of the church that has its' roots in an Old Testament concept that was established by God Himself. Like many of the church's teachings, when we look at it through the lens of Jesus Christ, we are able to see it and interpret it more clearly for our lives as Christians in the church of today. The word *Sabbath* literally means to *cease, stop* or *rest* in its original Hebrew form. So, when we read about the Sabbath in the Old Testament, our first exposure to it comes in Genesis 2 where the bible records that after finishing the work of creation in six days, God rested on the seventh day and declared it holy. One day out of every seven was to be a day of rest for human beings at which time we would mark and celebrate God finishing the creation of the physical world. While the Jewish Sabbath is traditionally celebrated on Saturday, the bible does not specifically name a day of the week. Rather it highlights that one day out of seven is to be set aside for Sabbath rest. God created the Sabbath for us, and has created us so that we may need the Sabbath.

In general, the bible teaches that humans are supposed to

rest on the Sabbath, cease their labor, and only perform deeds of necessity, mercy and worship. It was a day designed to replenish the mind, body and spirit within man. Jesus himself also observed the Sabbath, being a devout Jew; however by the time Jesus began His ministry on earth, Jewish religious teachers had devised and added more than 1500 rules of conduct designed to regulate the observance of the Sabbath. Therefore, the Sabbath eventually became more of a burden than a blessing. Jesus basically ignored these man-made rules but always kept the fourth commandment as God intended it to be observed. Jesus taught that the Sabbath was made for man, not man for the Sabbath. As is almost always the case, whenever human beings add man-made rules onto God's law, it usually ends up in a mess that deviates from what God wills and desires for us. So, Jesus declared that He was also Lord of the Sabbath. That means that we must understand Jesus and His mission and ministry to have a proper and complete understanding of what the Sabbath is supposed to be. Some of Jesus' most heated disagreements with the Pharisees and other religious leaders of His day were over what could or could not be done on the Sabbath.

In the New Testament, there is a distinct shift in the language of the bible that begins on the day of Resurrection of our Lord Jesus Christ. It is clearly recorded in scripture that Jesus arose on the "*first day of the week*". Therefore, as opposed to the Jewish Sabbath, which is Saturday, Jesus was crucified on Friday but arose on Sunday. Even Jesus' post-resurrection appearances to the disciples happened on the *first day of the week*. When the new early Christian church would gather for worship it was on the *first day of the week*. Later in the language and culture of the Christian church, it began to be referred to as the "*Lord's Day*".

So, we see how the Christian Sabbath has its history in the Old Testament establishment of the Jewish Sabbath as it was created by God and articulated in the Ten Commandments. But we also see how Jesus Christ has re-interpreted the meaning of the Sabbath for all of humanity and placed it in its proper perspective and meaning. Every Lord's Day, Sunday, the first day of the week is a day that incorporates all of the principles of rest and commemoration that we get from the Old Testament, and also adds the principles of blessing, celebration, service, mercy and worship that Jesus shows us in the New Testament. So as Christians, our Sabbath is traditionally celebrated every Sunday because Jesus' life, death and resurrection have redefined the meaning of the term "*Lord's Day*" for us. Jesus is Lord and Sunday, the first day of the week is His day of Resurrection! The Jewish Sabbath in the Old Testament and the Christian Sabbath of the New Testament complement each other in some remarkable ways; among them are the following:

1) Creation & Redemption

In the Old Testament, the Sabbath represented God's completion of creation. Everything in the physical world and ultimately human beings were all created by God. The Sabbath was God's day to rest, observe and contemplate all that He had created. Likewise, the Christian Sabbath on Sunday represents God redeeming all of creation from the fall and the effects of sin in the world. The resurrection of Jesus Christ on Sunday is the ultimate symbol of God's plan of redemption for humanity and all of creation. It is in fact like God is preserving, saving or re-creating all of His creation for His glory. As God rested from His creative work on the Old Testament Sabbath, He rests from His redemptive work at Calvary on the Christian Sabbath.

2) Rest & Contemplation/Service

The Old Testament Sabbath was one that encouraged rest from physical labor. The intent was to allow the body, mind and spirit to be replenished so that man could be effective in labor for the next six days. Rest is essential for human beings! God thought that rest was so important that He declared that the Sabbath was a holy day that we should observe every seven days. In the New Testament we see how we are not simply to rest physically, but that we should be using the time to meditate on God and consider God's presence in our lives and how He wants us to work. It should be a time where we contemplate how we can live better during the next week and glorify God even more in our lives. The rest that God designed for us on the Old Testament Sabbath gives us the sacred space in our lives on the Christian Sabbath to help us think about how we can be more like Jesus Christ in our daily lives; by showing mercy, love, justice and service to our fellow man. It is a time of personal meditation and devotion.

3) Recognition & Celebration/Worship

The Old Testament Sabbath was also a special way of recognizing God and acknowledging God as the One who has authority to order our daily lives. God's declaration of the Sabbath day as holy sets a certain tone for every day of the week. Likewise, the Christian Sabbath is the day that we go to church for the purpose of worship. In the act of worship we express to God how much we love Him and what He is "worth" to us. Every Sunday is a day of celebration when we gather to experience worship in the church. We are celebrating the reality that God is our God, that Jesus is our Lord, and that the Holy Spirit gives us power to be the church that God created us to be. We do it out of obedience and because of the joy that God gives us in our relationship to Him and each other.

Reader's Remix:
Real-life Reflections on Chapter Six

Do you partake regularly in the Lord's Supper / Communion? Do you observe the Sabbath through rest, reflection, and worship? These are simple disciplines in life that can bring us all closer to God and his Will. Understanding our place in the Baptist Church is paramount to being active in that community and contributing as true, active Believers. Reading and digesting these particular Articles of Faith is step one in gaining knowledge regarding our specific responsibilities; step two is up to us. Do we continue to passively worship on Sunday or do we begin to actively understand God and His plan for us? Do we truly remember how Jesus died on the cross for us when we take communion or do we just see it as something we do when we attend services?

Part of what we've discussed, thus far, involves reading these Articles and digesting them, but... more importantly, applying them directly to our lives as we move forward in this life. This is the conscious step we must take in becoming more informed Christians.

Chapter 7

How Does Civil Government Fit With it All?

Article XVI. CIVIL GOVERNMENT

Psalm 22:28; Proverbs 8:15; Isaiah 9:6-7; Jeremiah 1:9-10
Matthew 22:15-22; Romans 13:1-7; Ephesians 6:11-12

The traditional interpretation of the Articles of Faith:

We believe the Scriptures teach that civil government is of divine appointment, for the interest and good order of human society; and that magistrates are to be prayed for, conscientiously honored and obeyed; except only in things opposed to the will of our Lord Jesus Christ, who is the only Lord of the conscience, and the Prince of the Kings of the earth.

REMIXED:

We believe that governmental officials on all levels are supposed to be servants who are appointed and affirmed by God to serve and maintain order in human society. God is sovereign over all government leaders, and Christians should pray for those who occupy political positions of leadership on all levels. Christians are both heavenly citizens and earthly citizens; and just as we are accountable for following God's law, we should also respect the law of the land. If the law of the land is unjust, then we must work as agents of change and transformation empowered by God to change the law and the positions of governmental leaders as appropriate.

This doctrinal teaching of the church reminds us that as people of God we have *dual citizenship*. That is, we are *heavenly citizens* in the Kingdom of God because of the salvation that we have received through Jesus Christ, but we are also still *earthly citizens* who live in this world and must, therefore, live with governmental structures that exist in our community, city, state and nation. If we are not careful, there is a strong temptation to think that because we are Christians, we don't have to be concerned about the law of the land where we live physically as much. However, this article of faith teaches us that as Christians we do have a responsibility to be good citizens, follow the law, and be in critical dialogue with the civil government structures that affect us. As people of God, we understand that government and the elected and appointed government officials who serve are entities that are established as instruments in God's plan. God rules above all governments in the world, so government officials and politicians should understand that they are accountable to God for how they use the power and influence associated with their office. Government exists as a way of serving and protecting people, and God desires to use government and government officials in that way. Unfortunately, though, some in government tend to forget this divine accountability and instead fall into the tragic trap of *playing politics* instead of serving people as God would have them do. In instances such as this, it is the calling and responsibility of God's people to hold them accountable and critique and correct this government gone wrong, if you will. And, if necessary, God's people can and should engage in acts of *civil disobedience* in order to bring about change and transformation if government is not functioning in agreement with God's will and ways. To engage in civil disobedience, as citizens of this world and of the Kingdom of God, those wishing to create productive change must act with Godly wisdom and courage. Any acts need to be administered with the right motive which seeks justice for all people, especially those who are oppressed or marginalized in the community. Only in this way will both positive social or political change occur and God's will can be satisfied and followed. Those who harm or act irresponsibly are not acting in God's name – even those in positions of power like our civic, political, and other leaders.

If we read the bible closely and critically, we will note that God's people have had to grow and evolve in the midst of times and places where government functioned in both Godly and ungodly ways. Often God used a chosen person to critique government and bring about social change. In the Old Testament, Moses and the children of Israel clashed with Pharaoh and the Egyptian government. When Israel became its own nation, God called prophets like Nathan, Isaiah, Jeremiah, Elijah and Elisha to confront the kings and the government that they ran when they were going against God's will. During the Exile, God used Daniel and the three Hebrew boys to disobey unrighteous laws by the kings of Babylon and eventually change the laws of the land.

In the New Testament, we see clearly how Jesus is referred to as King of the Jews and King of Kings and how that creates conflict with Herod, Pilate and eventually Caesar. We also know that Paul clashed with the government of his day and appealed to have his case heard by Caesar in Rome. Throughout the book of Acts we see how the disciples were beaten, thrown in jail and abused by the government officials at the time because they were proclaiming Jesus Christ.

In more recent history, we know how many brothers and sisters such as Mahatma Gandhi, Martin Luther King, Jr., and many others who engaged in acts of civil disobedience in the civil rights movement in the USA, and in many other movements around the world have had to confront government for the sake of righteousness.

As Christians we are responsible for being good citizens and obeying the law, but we are also equally responsible for critiquing government and holding it accountable when it is not operating in a way that is consistent with God's will. Regarding this issue of civil government, it is important for us to remember the following:

1) Governments are established by God and are accountable to God

Government structures and those who work in government exist there by the grace of God. God holds them accountable for serving humanity in a way that reflects His will and His way. Government officials and politicians will be held accountable by God for the way that they have used their offices, respectively. The laws that government establishes should be for the good of all and Christians are supposed to obey the law. When we obey the law, we are being a good witness for Jesus Christ in our communities. So, we should respect government and the laws that it establishes because God is above all governments and intends to work through them to protect and serve people.

2) We should sincerely pray for all government officials.

Those who work in any level of government have a tremendous responsibility and burden to carry. From the President of the United

States to the local community public servant, everyone who works in government is regularly tempted to misuse or abuse the authority of their office for a number of different purposes. God's people should pray earnestly for all government officials so that they will stay grounded and focused on God's desire and will for how their position, power and influence should be used.

3) When necessary, we must critique government and work to change it

Like Daniel and the prophets in the Old Testament, Jesus and Paul in the New Testament, and Dr. Martin Luther King Jr. and our mothers and fathers in the civil rights movement in this country, we must engage in acts of civil disobedience, protest and dialogue when government is operating in an ungodly way. The prophetic critique and ministry that runs throughout the bible is a part of our calling too. As Christians, we must not be afraid to speak truth to power and work for social change when we see unrighteousness in our communities and nation. This does not mean we are disrespecting the law, rather it means that in God's sight, the particular law or practice itself is in fact unjust; therefore, we are respecting the law by transforming it into a righteous law or practice. God used people to do this all throughout the bible, and that prophetic calling must continue with us in the church today.

It is our job to hold ourselves, our neighbors, and, yes, those in power politically, socially, and economically to certain ethical, God-fearing standards. It isn't always easy, but it is one of our responsibilities as Christians.

Reader's Remix:
Real-life Reflections on Chapter Seven

Most people think that church and state are separate. Most governments are structured so that one does not interfere with the other and laws are worded and executed carefully so that no one is discriminated against at this level – even nonbelievers, agnostics, and atheists. This is why it is often difficult to remember that we do have a responsibility to others in a Godly way on every level.

When politicians misbehave or misrepresent the people or their office, it is our responsibility to speak out. In fact, it is wrong to ignore policies that discriminate, exclude, and even abuse certain demographics. It is wrong to ignore police brutality and lewd behavior in offices that should be held to certain standards. We cannot turn our head, complain, and plod on with our daily lives. It is our job to hold ourselves, our neighbors, and, yes, those in power politically, socially, and economically to certain ethical, God-fearing standards. It isn't always easy, but it is one of our responsibilities as Christians.

Chapter 8

The Righteous, the Wicked, and the World to Come

Article XVII. RIGHTEOUS AND WICKED

Matthew 25:31-46; Romans 14:10-12; 2 Corinthians 5:10; Hebrews 9:27-28

The traditional interpretation of the Articles of Faith:

We believe the Scriptures teach that there is a radical and essential difference between the righteous and the wicked; that such only as through faith are justified in the name of the Lord Jesus, and sanctified by the Spirit of our God, are truly righteous in his esteem; while all such as continue in impenitence and unbelief are in his sight wicked, and under the curse; and this distinction holds among men both in and after death.

REMIXED:

We believe that there is a distinct difference between good and evil in the world. There are righteous people and wicked people in the world, and there is also a heaven and a hell. God is the one who has authority to judge between the two, and the difference is whether or not a person has a relationship or connection with God. Those who reject God and rebel against God's will are the wicked, and their works are evil in the world because they are ungodly and against the message of the Gospel of Jesus Christ. A time will come when God will judge between the righteous and wicked, and each will receive the reward or consequences associated with the life they have lived in this world.

This scriptural teaching is one that is often difficult for many in this post-modern age to accept or embrace. When contemporary thinkers look at this doctrine, they have a tendency to label it as "*judgmental*" or "*intolerant*". Perhaps it is because one of the trademarks of the post-modern era is that everything is "*relative*", and nothing is really definitely black or white, but, rather, everything is really shades of gray. In post-modern thinking, there is no real absolute truth, no absolute right or wrong and really no absolute good or bad. Everything is simply relative based on the perspective of the individual – even in determining what is wicked and what is righteous behavior.

This doctrinal teaching tells us that scripture teaches us that from God's perspective there is a distinct difference between the righteous and the wicked, between right and wrong, and between heaven and hell. And the point is that God Himself is the judge who determines and declares us to be one or the other. Judgment is not in the hands of individuals, rather God is the only and the ultimate judge who declares us righteous. The righteous are those who have been saved by Jesus Christ, justified by God and sanctified by the Holy Spirit of God. The wicked are those who have chosen to reject and resist the message and invitation of God that has been presented to them in the Gospel of Jesus Christ. When a righteous person dies, he or she is rewarded with eternal life in fellowship with God and all other believers in heaven. When a wicked person dies, he or she is subject to the consequences of the curse, which occurred in the Fall of Man, and, thus, he or she is dismissed from the presence of God to spend eternity in hell.

All human beings will be judged by God based on how we have

lived in this life. This is all the more reason why we should be so thankful for Jesus Christ! We are saved from an eternal punishment in hell because Jesus Christ has redeemed us and made our lives brand new. There is a heaven and a hell.

After we have lived our appointed time on earth, we must all stand before God to be judged, and then we will spend eternity in either heaven or hell. Thank God that He has provided the way for us to have everlasting life with Him through Jesus Christ. This we have examined at length in the previous Articles of Faith.

There are many who don't believe that there is a heaven or hell, or that God will judge us. But scripture is clear in pointing out that God is watching how we live, and that He distinguishes between what and who is good and evil, righteous or wicked (2 Corinthians 5:10). We are all far from being perfectly holy on our own, but, as Christians, we must always strive to become more and more like Jesus each day. We will have to give an account to God one day for how we have lived in this life. Thank God for grace! We believe that Jesus is coming back again, and when He comes back again, He is coming to judge the world and everybody in it. We don't know when He is coming back or when we may die, so it behooves us to live each day to the glory of God and to try to please the Lord with every moment of life that we have.

We don't know when He is coming back or when we may die, so it behooves us to live each day to the glory of God and to try to please the Lord with every moment of life that we have.

Article XVIII. THE WORLD TO COME

Matthew 24:3-14; 1 Corinthians 15:50-58;
1 Thessalonians 4:13-18; Revelation 21:1-6

The traditional interpretation of the Articles of Faith:

We believe the Scriptures teach that the end of the world is approaching, that at the last day, Christ will descend from heaven, and raise the dead from the grave for final retribution; that a solemn separation will then take place; that the wicked will be adjudged to endless punishment, and the righteous to endless joy; and that this judgment will fix forever the final state of men in heaven or hell, on principles of righteousness.

REMIXED:

We believe that God has a time and a way for this world as we know it to come to an end and give way to God's new creation of a new heaven and a new earth. No man knows the day or the hour when this time will come, that knowledge is held by God alone. It is our responsibility to live each day in anticipation of God's plan and using the time responsibly to spread God's message throughout the world. When this new world comes, Jesus will return as a King to judge the world and those in it, and God will reign forever.

In this article of faith we see that God has a divine plan for humanity and all of creation that will culminate in accordance with God's will. Creation and this world is not just a project that God started without knowing where and how it will all end. On the contrary, God has a time and a way for this world as we know it to come to an end and give way to God's new creation, which we refer to as the *world to come*. In the language of the church, we refer to this subject as *eschatology*, which means the study of the last things, the end of the age, and the culmination of human history as we know it.

For years, we have been having conversations in the church about how we are living in the "latter days" or the "last days" because the signs that we see in our daily culture seem to be fulfilling a lot of the prophecy that the bible talks about when the last days are described. Generally, when we talk about the last days, we are referring to the time leading up to that day when Jesus Christ comes back into the world to judge the world and bring it to its' culmination before God creates a new heaven and earth. Yes, we believe that God will create another world to come in which Satan and all of his influence has been defeated, and the Lord will reign forever.

We have also heard many rumors and predictions about when the world is going to end, and when Jesus is coming back. False prophets have risen up and made bold statements claiming to know the time when the end of the world is coming. There were even those who believed that the Y2K issue, when we had to rely on all systems in this computer age to recognize the year 2000 without fail, was a signal of the end of the world! Jesus talked about these false predictors and warned us not to believe them. The point is that no one but God knows the day or time when Jesus is coming back or when the world is coming to an end. It is our responsibility to make sure that we live each day for Christ so that we are ready whenever the day comes! The point is not to predict the time, but to live every moment in accordance with God's will so that we are always prepared for His coming.

While there are many who are still making predictions by trying to interpret the meaning of the prophecy in the bible, the best thing for us to do is to live by our faith in God. We don't know when Jesus is coming back, but the important thing is that we believe that He is coming back. Therefore, we live each day in expectation, looking for our savior and ready to receive His coming with joy. We should always remember that:

1) Jesus is coming back again!

2) When Jesus comes back, He will judge the world.

3) God is going to create a new heaven and earth where God reigns forever!

Reader's Remix:
Real-life Reflections on Chapter Eight

These last Articles of Faith are problematic ones in that it is exceedingly difficult, as individuals, to evaluate our own behavior. Further, it is often difficult to change or modify behavior from wicked to righteous. And, of course, beyond that, it is often very hard to imagine the end of time – our judgment day. Obviously, then, it is tough to determine how to live at times. Are we just in our treatment of other people? Are we fulfilling God's plan for us on a daily basis? Are we good Christians? Do we understand our faith, Baptist or other?

In examining all the Articles of Faith and our role in translating them to a faithful Christian life, we must, first, examine our own existence as Christians and citizens of this world.

> ***We must determine whether or not we are living a full life – a Godly life – and, across the board, behaving as human beings who love, give, and never turn away from those in need.***

We must determine whether or not we are living a full life – a Godly life – and, across the board, behaving as human beings who love, give, and never turn away from those in need.

Educating ourselves in scripture and, further, truly understanding it all in a way that allows us to teach through words and by example is one way to prepare for a greater level of service to God. It is another way to live as Jesus did – teaching, loving, and remaining faithful to His responsibilities as prophet and savior.

As informed, willing Christians, we can change this world. By understanding and nourishing our belief system, we can further the role of Christians, regardless of denomination, in this world. Ask yourself now, before we move on to an expanded examination of our beliefs – do I understand myself and my relationship to God? Do I serve God? Do I really embrace the Articles of Faith? And, once again, am I a faithful Christian?

PART II.

What Else Do We Believe?

Chapter 9

How We Really Live Beyond the Articles of Faith

Addendums To What We Believe

The Articles of Faith, as a document, is one example of a good framework for us to use as we learn how to articulate what we believe and why; however, the Articles of Faith are not all-inclusive of everything that we may talk about or need to know concerning the church. Indeed, one of the effects of post-modernity on the church of today is that we emphasize different things and certainly ask different questions than we used to in the church twenty or more years ago. Now, we want to know why there are different worship styles. We want to know how to pray. And, we have other loftier questions like: Is church membership the same as discipleship? This reality reflects the fact that God is still moving and speaking within human history and the church.

As any observant theologian knows, as times change and culture changes, the church then must also necessarily change and adapt its paradigms and patterns in order to remain relevant to the needs of people and communities in this present age. We must ask ourselves relevant questions that apply to modern life like: What are the most effective methods for doing evangelism in today's busy world? How should we be involved with social justice issues? And, on a personal level; what does God expect of me regarding my money? In my conversations with both clergy and laity, it occurred to me that there are some topics that are of great significance to us currently in the church that are indirectly addressed in tangential ways in the articles of faith, but are not directly engaged in theological discourse the way they should be. In essence, there are certain topics and issues that are prevalent in the church of today that deserve their own article of faith such as missions or social justice ministry, especially given the current cultural climate that we live in and the challenges that the church faces daily.

If I were to ever have the opportunity to write a new version of the Articles of Faith from my unique perspective and paradigm, there are some points that would certainly be included as important doctrinal issues worthy of their own individual article. It is quite probable that when the traditional Articles of Faith are taught and discussed with depth and intentionality, these issues would surely arise in some form. For example, the issue of social justice may arise when certain pastors presented the Article of Faith on Civil Government to their congregations. However, I am simply arguing that these issues, including **worship, prayer, discipleship, missions, evangelism, stewardship, spiritual gifts,** and **social justice ministry,** are close enough to the forefront of issues in the church today that they warrant an intentional inclusion in the doctrinal teaching of the church. Certainly this list is not exhaustive or all encompassing, but it is, currently, what I have observed to be important issues in the church based on conversations with both laity and clergy. When new members are indoctrinated into the teachings of the church, in addition to the Articles of Faith, these are topics about which they should be educated in order to make the church more effective in its ministry and mission and to help these new and old members to be theologically- grounded personally while on their respective faith journeys.

While there is no officially proposed article for each topic in the following section, the presentations represent biblical lessons that can be taught in the church in order to help laity and clergy begin to understand how these issues are grounded biblically and theologically as well as what the practical implications are of each.

Chapter 10

Worship, Prayer and Discipleship

"What is Worship?"

Deuteronomy 5:6-10, Psalm 95:1-6, Psalm 150
Matthew 14:29-33, Matthew 15:21-25, John 4:20-24, Acts 17:22-28, Hebrews 10:23-25

The word "worship" in the Bible generally translates to mean "to give reverence, respect, or to pay homage to someone or something with an attitude of humility". As Christians, we understand that we are to worship God only, first and foremost, and, since Jesus Christ is God in the form of human flesh, and the Holy Spirit is the living, active power of God in the world, our worship must necessarily include the Lord Jesus Christ and the Holy Spirit in our worship experiences – the whole Holy Trinity.

In general, when we worship we are expressing to God what He is "worth" to us. When we worship, we are doing more than just acknowledging or noticing the existence of God; we are reverencing God and expressing our sincere homage to Him as our Creator, Sustainer and all-powerful God. Worship is a personal and communal choice that we make as individuals and, as a church, to actively and intentionally express our reverence and adoration to God while in His presence. The real key to understanding what a truly authentic worship experience is lies in understanding that God is the most important focal point of worship, not us! Unfortunately, there are those who seek to make worship *services* in church about us as human beings. It appears that we want church services to be about *our* desires, *our* preferences, *our* wishes and attention focused on *us*. But that is not what true worship is all about. Worship is not just a service; it is an *experience* of being in the presence of the Almighty God and giving

Him reverence and praise. It is not the service or the order of service that makes worship real; the services are just our plans and guides. What makes worship real is the fact that God the Father is present, the Lord Jesus Christ is present, and the Holy Spirit is present! God is always the most important person present in any worship experience. When we understand this reality, it can and should change the attitude with which we approach worship in the church. Regarding worship, it is important to remember the following:

We show that we understand that God is God, and that we are not God

What is worship?

Simply speaking, worship is an experience in which we are intentionally in the presence of God for the purpose of expressing our reverence, respect, homage, adoration and praise to God. God is the most important focal point of any true worship experience, and true worshippers approach worship with the intention of expressing this reality to God through words, actions, thoughts and deeds. Worship is the intentional experience during which we express to God what He is "worth" to us. Worship is the intentional experience and space where we show God that we understand what our relationship to God is. We show that we understand that God is God, and that we are not God. We show God that we know for ourselves that God is worthy of praise, honor, respect and reverence.

Why do we worship?

We worship God because He is worthy of our worship. God is

worthy of our worship first of all **because of who God is.**

God is the Creator, Sustainer, Redeemer and Liberator of all mankind and all of creation. God is eternal, omnipotent, omniscient, omnipresent and awesome in all of His attributes and character. Secondly, we worship God because of **what God has done**. We worship because we are thankful for what God has done for us, **what He is doing right now**, and for what **He has promised to do for us.** We worship because God's character and God's activity cause feelings of gratitude to emanate from us, and the proper response to God for that is to worship Him. We can never repay God for who He is and what He has done; therefore, our proper response should be to be obedient to what God has commanded us to do. That response is to worship Him alone and have no other gods in our lives. We worship because the acts and attitudes of sincere worship cause us to focus in on God and to be in His presence.

We worship God because
He is worthy of our worship.

When and Where do we worship?

The most obvious answers to these questions are that we worship on the Lord's Day, Sunday, and we worship in the church building. While both of these answers are correct, they are not the only answers. The Bible is clear in telling us to honor the Lord's Day by worshipping and to assemble ourselves together as a church family for the purpose of worship. Coming together as a church family on Sundays for worship is indeed necessary and important, and God expects us to do it regularly and consistently. But the Bible also has instances where individuals worshipped alone or in small groups and, additionally, people worshipped in places outside the church like in the streets, on a boat, in the community, etc....So we can see that worship is supposed to take place in the church, but, more importantly, that it is a constant disposition and attitude that we should have all of the time in life wherever we are and, therefore, can and should occur anywhere. We should be in a

continual posture of worship in our attitude toward God everyday and anywhere we go. This is NOT a substitute for coming to church and worshipping as a church family; the premise to be mindful of worship in every aspect of our lives is simply meant to encourage us to add onto that worshipping foundation and carry it outside of the church building with us everywhere we go including our homes.

How do we worship?

The Bible records many different ways that people worshipped God. The first and earliest acts of worship that occur in the Bible are the acts of giving an offering and a tithe. Cain and Abel brought their offerings to God, while Abraham paid tithes back in the book of Genesis. Long before church as we know it today, the first acts of worship involved giving sacrificially to God. Beyond that, other acts of worship throughout the Bible include the following: Preaching, prayer, singing, playing musical instruments, meditation, dance, physical movements, lifting up hands, standing, praising, the sacraments (communion & baptism) and reading scripture. All of these are acceptable forms of worship in the Bible, and God received them. After all, worship must be received by God. God judges what are acceptable forms of worship; we do not judge. They were done both privately and publicly, both personally and congregationally. In either case, God always looks at the sincerity of the person's heart more than He does the outside show. We always do our best in preparing and planning to worship, however God is most concerned that we worship in spirit and in truth above all else.

"What is Prayer?"
2 Samuel 7:27-29; 2 Kings 20:1-3; 2 Chronicles 7:13-16;
Psalm 5:1-3;Psalm 55:16-17; Psalm 122:6; Daniel 6:10
Matthew 6:5-15; Matthew 17:18-21; Mark 11:22-26; Luke 18:1;
John 14:13-14; John 17:9-21; Acts 12:1-5; Romans 8:26;
1 Thessalonians 5:17; James 5:13-18; 1 Peter 3:7

Prayer is an act of worship and a spiritual discipline in which we communicate and commune with God. When we pray, we are humbly approaching God with our prayer concerns so that we can tell God about them. It is not that God does not already know what is going on in our lives, but as the Bible teaches us, we often *"have not because we ask not"*. It is a wonderful blessing and privilege that God has given to all of His people to be able to go to God in prayer. We have this access to talk to the almighty omnipotent God because of Jesus Christ. No longer do we have to go through a priest like the Levites of the Old Testament when it was believed that people, unworthy themselves, had to rely on a priest or religious leader to pray for them. Because of Jesus Christ, our great High Priest, we now have access to God directly as His children, and we can pray to God and talk to God for ourselves. When Jesus died on the cross and was resurrected from the dead, He became the perfect, complete sacrifice for our sins. Therefore, we can now approach God confidently because the sacrifice of Jesus Christ covers us and makes us worthy to approach the awesome God of the universe.

Thank God for prayer! We can talk to God about what is on our heart regarding any and everything in our lives. Our joys and sorrows, our triumphs and tragedies, our victories and vices are all things that we reference and discuss in prayer.

It is also important to remember that prayer is not just simply a time for us to do all the talking. If prayer is a time when we commune and communicate with God, then it is also important for us to spend time listening to God when we pray. Prayer is two-way communication between God and us. We should spend quality time in prayer to tell God about what's in our heart, and we should also spend time listening as God tells us what is in His heart for us as He speaks to us through the Holy Spirit.

Prayer is two-way communication between God and us.

So, prayer is not simply the act of repeating the neat, concise prayers that we memorized as children for bedtime or grace before we eat! Prayer is a daily spiritual discipline in which we are engaging in quality conversation and communion with God. It should also be noted that prayer is something that can happen both *personally and corporately*. In other words, each individual Christian should have a personal prayer life in which we talk to God ourselves everyday as a part of our personal daily devotional life as well as a prayer life in church where we worship as a community. In this way, we are working on our own personal relationship to God. But we should also partake in a *corporate* prayer life when we join with other Christians in the church congregation, in small groups, and with prayer partners to touch and agree on one accord and pray for various concerns together. Both personal and corporate prayer are important in the life of a Christian, and we should do both regularly and consistently.

When we are in worship as a church family on Sunday mornings, we are praying corporately as a church family together. In the prayer of invocation, we are acknowledging God's presence in the church, and celebrating and welcoming His presence and movement in the worship experience. In the altar prayer, we are bringing our prayer concerns and requests to the altar and putting them in God's hands under His authority. The act of coming to the altar symbolizes that we are turning them over to God and leaving them at the place of sacrifice and worship.

It is important to also note that a Christian's prayer life can be hindered by our own actions or lack thereof. The Bible teaches us that un-forgiveness in our heart toward someone can hinder our prayers from being heard by God. We also see that when husbands mistreat their wives in the marriage relationship, it can hinder their prayers, for example. While it is not directly stated in 1 Peter 3, given the context of scripture as a whole as it relates to marriage in that it is a mutual and respectful relationship, we can also surmise that this applies to wives mistreating their husbands as well. Clearly, these examples from scripture illustrate how personal life directly affects our relationship with God and our private prayer life, in general.

As it relates to the issue of prayer in general, it is important to remember the following:

1) How do I pray?

Jesus gives us what we call the *"Lord's Prayer"* or the *"Model Prayer"* in the New Testament. While this prayer is in fact what Jesus taught, we must remember that it is not the *only* prayer that He prayed or taught. Jesus also taught the importance of praying about what is in your heart sincerely and not just praying to be seen and perceived well by others. And this is easy; in fact, we can pray by simply telling God what our concerns are in the most sincere way that we know. The Bible also speaks of some who may have the gift of praying in an unknown tongue, but if a Christian does not have that gift, he or she can still pray in his or her own words as long as it is, as we established earlier, sincere and heartfelt. One of the simplest formulas for understanding how to pray is "ACTSI", which stands for adoration, confession, thanksgiving, supplication and intercession. Additionally, it is important to remember that Christians should pray *"in the name of Jesus."* When we pray in the name of Jesus, we are acknowledging the will of God in our prayers and ensuring that our prayers are not simply self-centered or self-serving. Prayer is supposed to bring us closer to God's will, not to improve or boast our own.

2) How long should I pray?

Christians should pray every day for the rest of our lives in all seasons of our lives. In fact, the bible teaches that we should *"pray without ceasing"* and that we should *"always pray and not faint"*. This means that prayer is a consistent attitude, disposition and lifestyle that we should adopt as Christians. Aside from the intentional time that we spend in personal prayer and corporate prayer, Christians should be *prayerful* as people of God at all times and in every life experience.

3) What should I pray for?

We can and should pray for and about anything that is appropriate to ask for in Jesus name. Specifically, we see in the Bible that Jesus and other believers in the Old and New Testament prayed for: Healing, protection, guidance, deliverance, blessing of a house, blessing for a nation, leaders, God's intervention, encouragement, strength, to be kept from evil, forgiveness, God's movement, provision of food, to resist temptation, even your enemies, and much more. Surely, we as sincere, concerned, and devout Christians can pray for something similar.

"What is Discipleship?"
Matthew 28:19-20; Luke 9:23-25; Luke 14:25-35; John 8:31-32; Acts 11:25-26

When we use the term *"discipleship"* in the church, we are referring to the process by which people are developed and nurtured to become true disciples of Jesus Christ by another mature disciple of Jesus Christ so that they can then in turn nurture and teach someone else to become a disciple of Jesus Christ. A *"disciple"* is a learner. It is someone who has committed himself or herself to learning and living according to the teachings of another, usually a mentor of some kind. For us in the church, we are to be disciples of Jesus Christ.

A disciple is more than just a believer, a convert, or a church member. A person may believe in the existence of Jesus and even join the church, but that is no guarantee that he or she is a committed disciple. The devil and demons also know that Jesus is real, but they certainly don't live as His disciples! A disciple is called to live beyond church membership, denominational membership, or intellectual and theological knowledge of God. Disciples are people who embrace the teaching and life example of Jesus Christ and willfully commit to living by them and following them at all costs!

Discipleship is not a wishy-washy sometime choice that we make. It is a radical commitment where we are totally sold out to live for Jesus Christ and live like Jesus Christ under any and all life circumstances. So, we must confess that not every church member is a disciple, and every Christian is not even a disciple. There are many even in the body of Christ who will profess their belief in Jesus, but have not committed to fully living by His teaching.

Disciples are people who embrace the teaching and life example of Jesus Christ and willfully commit to living by them and following them at all costs!

Jesus constantly calls all of us to lives of Discipleship and then commands us to make more disciples in the world. Jesus Christ, Himself, was and is the greatest disciple-maker ever. His entire earthly life and ministry was a living example and lesson of what a true disciple is supposed to be. Everything that He did and said had some lesson within it that was communicating some truth about what it means to be a disciple. When Jesus died and ascended into heaven, the assignment that He left for His disciples and His church was to make more disciples for Him. So, the church cannot be content with just simply adding more members to its membership roster. The real work of the church is to teach and nurture people to become true disciples of Jesus Christ.

Jesus constantly calls all of us to lives of Discipleship and then commands us to make more disciples in the world.

So, as disciples of Jesus Christ, we are called first to be followers of Him in every dimension of our lives and then to replicate that process by teaching someone else to do the same. A disciple is someone who must constantly be striving to become mature in his or her faith and spiritual life. Disciples are constantly learning, constantly growing and maturing to become more and more like Jesus in every way. A disciple knows that there is always more to learn about God and God's word, so the disciple never feels like he or she has "arrived" or has learned all that there is to know; disciples know that learning is an ongoing process. Disciples are continually striving to be more and more like Jesus every day, and they are always looking for ways that they can help other believers make the transition from membership to discipleship.

It is important to note that the Great Commission found in

Matthew 28:19-20 more accurately translates in the NIV and other translations of the Bible to say "*go and make disciples of all nations, baptizing them in the name of the Father and of the Son and of the Holy Spirit, and teaching them to obey everything I have commanded you.*" Where the KJV says "teach all nations…", it is indeed more accurately translated to "make disciples" in other versions.

Jesus was and is our ultimate example of how to live like a disciple, and also how to make disciples. When you look at how Jesus taught the 12 apostles in the Bible and developed them into men who could carry the Gospel all over the world, it is impressive indeed. He was constantly teaching and modeling true discipleship for them to see firsthand. In fact, the disciples eventually came to be known as "Christians" because their lives reflected Jesus so much that the community began to see Jesus in them. That's the greatest compliment that a disciple could ever receive, that someone sees Jesus in us! Additionally, it is interesting to note that the early believers were disciples first, and then later became known as Christians. In other words, discipleship preceded the title "Christian", so true Christians are those who are first serious about discipleship and learning to be better and stronger in whatever endeavor they have chosen! If we are to be truly serious about discipleship in the church, we must consider the following:

1) **A disciple has set his or her life priorities on God, the way Jesus did, and lives it daily.**

2) **Disciples don't let worldly concerns distract them from doing the will of God.**

3) **Disciples not only love the Word of God, the Bible, but they live it daily.**

4) **A disciple has a servant's heart.**

5) **A disciple understands that becoming a disciple requires quality time daily and prayer.**

6) **A disciple is sensitive enough to invest time to help other disciples grow.**

7) **Disciples understand that they are constantly and continually learning about Jesus.**

Application for the Reader:
Reflections on Chapters Nine and Ten.

Our task as readers, Christians, those who study scripture and, yes, disciples is a bit of a daunting one after this section, isn't it? After all, we thought we knew how to worship, and now we learn that we may not know it all. We thought we knew how to pray, but we may not be doing enough. And, we thought we understood the term disciple, but it appears that, if we're not acting as disciples currently, we never had the whole story.

Can we learn from as well as mentor other Christians in our quest for further knowledge?

So, after being enlightened in the ways of focused and consistent daily worship, deep and respectful prayer, and a call to be disciples for God and the church, does it seem to be too much for us? Can we go forth and take our Sunday worship to the street – make God a part of our everyday lives? Can we make our simple prayers true dialogues with God everyday? Can we learn from as well as mentor other Christians in our quest for further knowledge? I think we all can; it just takes the conscious application of these ideas and practices to our daily grind – whether we're at home, at work, spending times with friends and family, or alone – we can do it. Jesus is our example.

Chapter 11

Missions, Evangelism, and Stewardship

"What is Missions?"

Matthew 25:31-46; Matthew 28:19-20; Mark 1:37-38; Luke 4:18-19; John 17:18, John 20:21; Acts 1:8; Acts 3:1-8; Acts 10:38; Acts 13:1-5; Acts 14:21-28; James 1:27

The word *missions*, or to be *missionary* refers to the basic fundamental work and identity of the church. In its purest sense, the church and all Christians are missionaries who are to engage in the work of the church, or missions, because God is our God, and He, Himself, is on a mission, if you will. Jesus

Christ is God, and He is the head of the church, or as we see in the Bible, the church is the body of Christ. So, therefore, if Jesus Christ is on a mission, then we in the church must also necessarily be on a mission as well. Mission is purpose, the reasons for the existence of whatever we hold valuable.

God is on a mission! We see this clearly in the life and ministry of Jesus Christ, and we can even see it in God's historical activity in the Old Testament. Truly, God has always been about having meaningful relationships with people – loving them, rescuing them, providing guidance to them, forgiving them, and providing for them – basically helping them reach their full potential and purpose. The Bible reveals to us that, ever since the Fall of Man, God has been on a mission to redeem humanity and all of creation. God has been on a mission to save people from the penalty of sin and reconcile them back to Himself. God accomplishes this mission in many different ways, some of which include spreading the Good News in the ministry of evangelism so that people will hear and respond to the message. But beyond that, God is concerned with the whole person. That is, He not only wants us to be changed spiritually, but God is also concerned with us physically, emotionally, mentally, socially and economically. In fact, one of the ways that God works to reconcile humanity back to Himself is by meeting human needs in all dimensions of our existence. This is the heart and soul of the true meaning of "Missions". God has called the church and all Christians to be involved in the ministry of meeting human needs so that people can see and experience the love of God through Jesus Christ.

One of the many reasons that God created the church was to live in the world and serve the world. So, wherever we see human needs or suffering, the church has the responsibility to respond to it. In that way, we are making the presence of God a reality to people who may not know Him. In Mission, the world is able to see that the church does actually practice what it proclaims. In Mission, the message of the Gospel that we proclaim becomes incarnate and alive to people. Mission and the ensuing work include the actions that the church does to minister to people at the point of their greatest need. Some of these actions include feeding the hungry, housing the homeless, clothing the naked, healing the sick, ministering to the incarcerated, liberating the captives, caring for the unwanted, helping the poor, educating the uninformed, loving the ostracized, serving the forgotten, preaching the gospel, protecting the vulnerable, and speaking for those who have no voice.

Mission is a large umbrella of responsibility for every Christian and every church; it encompasses the total task of ministry, which we are called to do in the name of Jesus Christ.

Mission is a call and command given by Jesus Christ to the

church in which we perform acts of ministry and service that are motivated by love, justice and peace and which serve to embody the reality of the kingdom of God here on earth. When you think about it in biblical terms, the idea of "missions" is truly a continuation of the ministry of Jesus Christ. The whole life and ministry of Jesus in the Bible is actual mission in action. And, therefore, the church takes up the work of missions because, as we established earlier, our God is on a mission. The church in the book of Acts is known for its evangelistic witness as well as its missionary work through preaching, teaching, baptizing, and healing in the communities. In fact, the apostle Paul is known to have become one of the strongest missionaries of the early church, and he led at least three missionary journeys. Because he was among the first to cross the cultural boundaries between Jews and Gentiles, Paul earned the distinction of being known as a *missionary to the gentiles.*

It has been suggested by biblical scholars that mission is the common thread that binds all of biblical history and theology together from both the old and new testaments. When you consider the stories of Adam, Noah, Abraham, Moses, Israel, Joshua, the Kings and Prophets, Jesus, the church and Paul, one can see that God has truly been on a mission throughout all of human history. Remember, Moses was chosen by God to lead the Israelites out of bondage and to provide for them in the wilderness, and Joshua led Israel to conquer and inherit the Promised Land where they were to settle and live as God said. God's desire has always been to meet human needs so that people can see Him more clearly and embrace Him.

God has called us to do this important work. Additionally, when we think about missions, we should note the following:

1) Every Christian is called to be a missionary.

God's original intent for the church and all Christians is that every church is a missionary church, and every Christian is a missionary. We are called and empowered by God to serve the world in this present age by meeting human needs wherever God enables us to see them. It is not only the responsibility of ministers or people who have devoted their lives to being missionaries on the mission field to do this work. God's purpose for us, both individually and as a church or community, is to be missionaries because Jesus was also a missionary. If a Christian takes his or her faith seriously, and if a church is to be truly faithful to Jesus Christ, then we must be actively involved in the work of missions. It is our identity and purpose as God intended.

2) We are called to do Home Missions.

Like Jesus in much of His ministry, and Peter and John in Acts 3, we are called to be missionaries in our local community. As people of faith, we must not neglect the needs of people that we see everyday around us in the community where we live. This is one of the key ways that communities get transformed. Acts of service for people locally introduces people to the love of Jesus Christ and helps them to feel His presence through us. This type of work is contagious and will impact communities in positive ways for God.

3) We are called to do Foreign Missions.

Like Jesus, the early church, and Paul, we are also called to be missionaries all over the world and to take this ministry to people outside of our local home community. In fact, anywhere that we see human need in the world, the church and all Christians are called by God to respond and serve people whether we know them or not. We believe that all people are created in the image of God, and that they deserve to feel the presence and love of God through acts of service that come from God's people in the church. So, we need to be missionaries to the whole world, and we need to cooperate with other Christians to be as effective as possible in this endeavor.

"What is Evangelism?"
Luke 4:18-19; John 4:25-30; Acts 2:38-42; Acts 8:35-40; Acts 16:25-34, Acts 17:6; Acts 21:8; Ephesians 4:11-15 , 2 Timothy 4:1-5

In simple terms, *evangelism* is the activity and ministry in which we tell people about the Good News of the Gospel of Jesus Christ, and invite them to embrace Him by faith and make Him Lord of their lives. The bible describes Christians as *evangelists*, meaning those who proclaim Good News. Evangelism is telling the story of Jesus Christ to those who may or may not have heard it before so that they can also share in the joy that we have as disciples of Jesus Christ. Evangelism is spoken or verbal communication during which we are purposely telling people about Jesus Christ and inviting them to receive Him into their lives.

The Good News that we proclaim when we evangelize is the death, burial, and resurrection of Jesus Christ and how He saves and brings new life to whoever believes in Him. We are motivated to share this good news with others because we realize how blessed we are to have Jesus Christ in our lives. The Gospel of Jesus Christ is good news for people as it relates to any and all areas of our lives. The only way that people in the world will know about it is if we who know the story tell it freely, openly and boldly wherever we go.

It is important to remember that evangelism is not just a church growth scheme or a marketing strategy used to attract people. It is definitely not simply about trying to increase numbers for the sake of profit. Evangelism is not simply the act of inviting people to church or to a particular denomination. Evangelism is also not a means to use fear to motivate people to join the church. Evangelism is a call and command given by Jesus Christ to the church and all Christians to share the Good News of the Gospel with all people. Evangelism is both a personal commitment and a corporate commitment by the church to be God's voices and mouthpieces in the world and to announce the reality of God's gospel message of salvation through Jesus Christ.

When we evangelize, we are primarily targeting people who are not yet believers in Jesus Christ, but we are also concerned about those who are already in the church but may not fully know God as they should. Therefore, evangelism involves both *outreach* and *inreach* so that all of us can become the disciples of Jesus Christ that God created us to be. When we evangelize, we are motivated by the love of God that we have experienced. So, if evangelism calls for us to go out of our way or cross some unusual barriers to share the gospel, we do it gladly because we realize what Jesus went through in order to save us! We also evangelize our family members, especially our children. We want to make sure that our children grow up to become adults who have faith in God and live for Jesus Christ. Of all of the things that we can pass on to our children, one of the most precious is faith in Jesus Christ!

Much has also been said about the "tele-evangelists" that are on television daily. There are many television ministries that are devoted to preaching and teaching the word of God for the purpose of leading people into a relationship with God through Jesus Christ. While some of these televangelists are sincere in their evangelistic purpose, we must be careful to discern between them and others who are involved in the work for other motives such as financial gain and greed. What is often missing from the ministry of televangelists is the follow-up discipleship and nurturing that must necessarily come after people have accepted Jesus Christ as a result of preaching and teaching. Additionally, true evangelism that proclaims the Good News of Jesus Christ is free of charge! The gospel is not for sale, and people should be able to hear it freely and without hindrances. Whether it is personal, one-on-one evangelism and witnessing; or in a congregational setting where there is a large crowd, evangelism is best done when people can receive the Word of God without barriers or pretenses.

When Christians evangelize in the world, we understand that it involves proclamation and invitation. We tell people the Good News and then invite them to receive and respond to the message that they just heard. That's what we are doing in worship services at church when we have the Invitation to Christian Discipleship; we are giving people the opportunity to respond to the gospel message in the sermon that was just preached. We always hope that someone who needs God in his or her life will accept the invitation and give his or her life to Jesus Christ. But we must always remember that people can either accept or reject the message; it is their choice. In authentic evangelism, our responsibility is to proclaim and invite, and God's work is to save and transform the person. Only God can truly save someone and change human nature. We don't have the ability to ultimately do that, but God does use our evangelistic efforts of telling the story and inviting people to receive it to complete the process.

For too long, Christians have been either too afraid or too timid to be evangelists as we should be.

For too long, Christians have been either too afraid or too timid to be evangelists as we should be. Perhaps one of the reasons that many Christians don't evangelize is because of the fear of rejection. We would rather give money to support it, or even let the preachers do it all as long as we don't have to do it ourselves. But God has not called us to be successful evangelists, just faithful and obedient. If we do our part, God is certainly able to do His part. Regarding evangelism, we must remember:

1) Every Christian is responsible for being an evangelist, not just preachers.

Every child of God who is saved has a testimony that can be used to evangelize someone. Sometimes the best evangelism is done by individuals in one-on-one settings or small groups. When was the last time you led someone to Jesus Christ? (Not just invite them to church)

2) God uses evangelism to dramatically change individual's lives.

Throughout the bible we see how individual experiences with someone who shared the good news changed a person's life forever. Jesus Himself was the greatest individual evangelist ever, and the early Christians followed His example.

3) God uses evangelism to dramatically change communities and the world.

The bible shows us how the early church changed entire cities and communities because of the way that they evangelized people. They are described as being people who have "turned the world upside down." The gospel of Jesus Christ has continued to go forth into the whole world, transforming cities, states, nations and continents. Evangelism changes the culture and climate of countries and ultimately the politics and leadership of nations. Evangelism is a powerful means of spreading God's message throughout the world!

"What is Stewardship?"
Psalm 24:1-2; Genesis 1:26-28; Haggai 2:8; Malachi 3:8-12
Luke 12:42; Luke 16:1-12; 1 Corinthians 4:1-2; Acts 4:32-35

The word "stewardship" refers to the responsibility of managing another person's property, finances, or business. Stewardship is a serious responsibility because the steward has been placed in a position in which he or she has been entrusted by the owner of the property, finances, or business to take care of these items as if they were his or her own. It is important for the steward to always remember that he or she does not own these items; he or she is only the caretaker, and they still belong to the owner! However, while the steward has them in his or her possession, they are to be managed and used so that they will multiply, grow, and otherwise be blessed; ultimately, the steward should be able to give a good report to the owner when the property is reclaimed.

Inherent in this point is another serious consideration for every steward; there will be a day of reckoning when the owner comes back to demand and account for the property that he or she has entrusted into the hands of the steward. The steward will then be judged on how well he or she has managed the owner's property. This judgment is based on what the owner thinks and not on what the steward thinks!

We are born into the world as stewards and created to be stewards over God's creation.

All human beings, particularly children of God, are stewards. We are born into the world as stewards and created to be stewards over God's creation. God is the owner of the world and all that He has created, and we are the stewards, entrusted with the care of this world. By far, the thing that so often causes Christians in the contemporary church to stumble over this issue of stewardship is the failure to properly distinguish between OWNERSHIP and STEWARDSHIP. God has ownership of everything in the world. God made the world before human beings were ever created; therefore, by virtue of that fact, He is undeniably the owner of everything. No human being can take credit or claim ownership of anything ultimately. Everything belongs to God, everyone belongs to God, and anything and anyone that will be belongs to God.

God created us in His image and likeness, and, in His infinite wisdom, God let human beings have "dominion" over all of His earth. As we established earlier, "dominion" means rule or responsibility to govern something. Dominion does not mean that we have ownership or that we can do as we please with creation. If God gave dominion, then God can take it back. This even extends to our money and financial/economic resources. Haggai lets us know that all of the financial riches and wealth of the world also belong to God, so our stewardship responsibility necessarily involves the way we handle our money. The tithe and the offering during worship at most churches are not only holy to God; they belong to God. It is not surprising, then, why Malachi (3:8) describes it as "robbing" God when we do not obediently give the tithe and offering to God's house.

As we look at the New Testament, we see that the concept of a steward is consistent, and that a spiritual dimension is added to it (Luke, Chapter 16, verses 1 – 12). Stewardship also describes the Christian's relationship to God. God is the owner, and we are God's servants, who are entrusted to be stewards not just over our own households, but over spiritual details such as the "Mysteries of God". So, basically, God has entrusted us, as Christians, to be stewards of His creations in a spiritual way in addition to the practical material or financial way. We are stewards of the Gospel message, the church, the ministry, the great commission regarding spreading the Gospel throughout the world, and of the love of God.

Traditionally, we have been taught that we are stewards over our TIME, TALENT and TREASURE. In other words, God has given us life, abilities and financial resources, and we need to remember that they all come from God. We are stewards of these attributes and blessings, and we should use them to the glory of God. Additionally, though, modern doctrinal teaching correctly points out that we are also stewards over creation, nature, the environment, our communities, organizations that we belong to, positions of responsibility that we have, and governments on all levels. We are stewards, not owners, and God is depending on us to manage His possessions in ways that please Him. We will give an account of our stewardship to God one day.

In general, we should do the following:

1) **We should worship God joyfully and obediently through giving tithes and offerings.**

2) **We should handle our possessions in ways that please God, not just ourselves.**

3) **We should use what God has given us to keep God's creation "good".**

4) **We should use what God has blessed us with to bless others.**

Chapter 12

Applying our Spiritual Gifts and Understanding Social Justice Ministry

"What are Spiritual Gifts?"
1 Corinthians 12:1-11 & 27-31; Romans 12:4-13; Ephesians 4:7-14; 1 Timothy 4:14; 1 Peter 4:10; 1 Corinthians 13:1-3

When we speak about spiritual gifts in the church, we are referring to the various divine abilities that the Holy Spirit distributes to every believer for the edification and good of the church. Every human being is born with certain natural abilities that God has created us with, but spiritual gifts are distinct from our natural abilities because they are uniquely designed to benefit the common good of the church and to further the cause of the Kingdom of God on earth. When spiritual gifts are exercised properly, they always glorify God and bear witness to the grace and goodness of God, whereas natural abilities tend to put the spotlight on the individual.

The spiritual gifts that God distributes to believers are found in the bible (1Corinthians 12: 1 – 11 and Romans 12: 4 – 13). They are consistent with the gifts that God gave to men and women in the bible days, and they are still relevant and effective for the church's mission and ministry today. We are admonished in the bible to be knowledgeable of our spiritual gifts; that is each individual should discern what spiritual gifts that he or she has been given because God does expect us to use them to the glory of God. In fact, we are accountable for the use or misuse of our spiritual gifts; they are a part of our stewardship responsibility as disciples of Jesus Christ.

It is critical that Christians discern and identify the spiritual gifts that God has given them because when we know our spiritual gifts, it helps us to operate and live within the purpose that God has for our lives in the church and in the world. God has a plan and purpose for every Christian's life. When God created us, He purposely and intentionally deposited certain gifts within us that are uniquely designed to help us in fulfilling our divine purpose. Just as individuals are different and unique, the combinations of gifts that God has put into every believer are unique as well. We don't all have the same gifts, and that is good because it causes us to have to work together and depend on each other in the body of Christ. As the bible teaches us, we are many members but one body. Different parts of the body have different purposes and functions, but all of the parts are necessary to make up the whole. So, each Christian is an essential part of the body of Christ and has a unique purpose in the church.

It should be noted that spiritual gifts are also different than the "*fruit of the Spirit*" as it is found in Galatians 5:22-23. The emphasis of the fruit of the spirit is on attributes that every believer should have in their daily walk with God after being filled by the Spirit. Spiritual gifts on the other hand, are specific activities that we do because God has gifted us in a certain way. The fruit of the Spirit is about "being" and Spiritual gifts are about "doing" as we live our daily lives. Spiritual gifts are however often related to our passion or zeal when it comes to serving God. Whenever we have a strong enthusiasm about a certain aspect of the work of the church, it may be an indication that we have gifts in a certain area. For example, those who are excited about having conversations with people about Jesus Christ very well may have the gift of evangelism. Additionally, we should also remember that we may have spiritual gifts in an area that we have yet to discover. As we continue to walk with God and live for Him, we sometimes find out that God reveals that we have certain spiritual gifts that we did not know about. So, we should always be open to new possibilities and opportunities that may come our way as we serve God in the church. It just may be that God is trying to use us in a new way to further the work of the church in the kingdom of God. In fact, some of us in the church may have the gifts of hospitality or leadership but have yet to discover them.

It is also important to know that all of our spiritual gifts, no matter what they may be, should always be used with love as our motivation. The biblical passage in 1 Corinthians 13 reminds us that no matter how gifted we may be, if we do not have love, it doesn't amount to anything. It is not enough for us to just be gifted or to even use our gifts for all to see; we must also do what we do with love in our hearts. This is commonly known as "agape" or God-like love that has all of the attributes that are described in the chapter such as patience, kindness, humility, and trust. A person can be gifted, and be actively using his or her gifts, but if this person is not working with love in his or her heart, harm, as opposed to good, can be done. In fact, if a person has the gift of administration but is not motivated by love, then the decisions that he or she might make in leadership could very well cause harm and division in the church and, inevitably, drive people away from the church family. If our gifts are not used with love as our motivation, then we could get the glory instead of God. Love is the key that binds all of the ministry and work of the church together in a way that makes it meaningful, effective, and pleasing to God.

Additionally, regarding spiritual gifts we should know the following:

1) Take the time to discover your own personal spiritual gifts.

Every disciple should pray and ask God to reveal to them what their gifts are. We can also ask our Pastor and other disciples who know us what gifts they see in us. We should also familiarize ourselves with what the spiritual gifts are as they appear in the bible. This list includes: administration, apostleship, craftsmanship, creative communication, discernment, encouragement, evangelism, faith, giving, healing, helps, hospitality, intercession, interpretation, knowledge, leadership, mercy, miracles, prophecy, shepherding, teaching, tongues and wisdom.

2) Remember that God made you unique and so are your gifts, you are valuable!

Every disciple of Jesus Christ in the church has at least one gift, and usually more than one. God created you with purpose and uniquely blessed you with the gifts that you have. You are not only precious in God's sight, but you are also an essential part of the church. You were created to bring Glory to God and to help the church to be faithful and effective in its ministry.

3) Know that the Kingdom of God and the church REALLY need you!

God gave each of us spiritual gifts to specifically further the work of the kingdom of God and the church. We are blessed so that we can be a blessing to someone else. You and your spiritual gifts are absolutely essential to helping the church be what God desires it to be. When Christians do not use their spiritual gifts for the church and allow them to lay dormant, the church suffers. It causes other Christians in the church to have to compensate for the absence of people who should be serving, and often forces them into areas of service that are outside of where their giftedness lies. That causes disciples to become burned-out and discouraged, and often less effective in the areas where their gifts actually are. So, the church needs everybody to do their part and use their gifts to the glory of God. The body needs all of its parts to truly function well!

"What is Social Justice Ministry?"
Leviticus 25:17; Deuteronomy 24:14-15; Psalm 82:1-4; Proverbs 21:2-3; Amos 5:24; Micah 6:8; Matthew 22:34-40; Luke 4:18-19; Luke 5:31; Galatians 3:28

Another very important part of our life of discipleship as Christians involves being a prophetic voice and witness in our society that calls for love, justice and peace. This calling comes from God and is demonstrated clearly in the lives of the Old Testament prophets such as Isaiah, Jeremiah, Amos, Micah, Malachi and others. It is also clearly illustrated in the ministry of Jesus Christ on earth. From their example, we see that social justice ministry involves a strong commitment to expose and confront social injustice that exists in the culture where we live, and that we should not only speak against it, but also work to change it.

When we look at the ministry of Jesus, the disciples, and the Old Testament prophets, we can see that in addition to addressing the spiritual needs of people; they also worked to break social barriers and obstacles of injustice and unfairness that people were often oppressed by. Sometimes it was economic injustice in which the rich were oppressing the poor. There were also times of political injustice, when kings and rulers were abusing their positions of authority and making unjust laws. There were also issues of racial injustice in which people were discriminated against based on their cultural background. One can also clearly notice incidents of gender bias and injustice toward women that reflect the cultural practices of the culture of that day. These biases and beliefs contradict one of the fundamental beliefs that we hold; all people are created in the image of God, and God loves all people. Whatever the case, God called and used men and women throughout the bible to set people free socially as well as spiritually. Whenever Jesus healed a leper or the woman with the issue of blood, or brought the widow's son back to life, or helped the blind to see and the lame to walk, we cannot ignore the fact that, along with being healed, these individuals were also restored socially in their communities, where, previously, they had been excluded and discriminated against. Based on our understanding of the kingdom of God, we believe that God intends for churches and communities to be places where people are treated with equality, justice, and love – not the opposite.

Jesus' teaching and parables about the Kingdom of God that talked about everyone being equal in the sight of God, and that God loves everybody furthers the cause of social justice ministry. Perhaps one of the best examples we have of this type of ministry in recent history is the leadership shown by the Black Church during the civil rights movement. Through leaders such as Martin Luther King, Jr. and others, God used people of faith to confront racism and other forms of social injustice and eventually change this nation. This type of ministry is consistent with the examples of the Old Testament prophets and Jesus Himself. Part of God's desire for humanity is that we love one another as He has loved us. We are to love God with all our hearts and also love our neighbor as ourselves. All human beings are our neighbors! So, therefore, we cannot say that we love our neighbors if we are also oppressing them economically, racially, socially, politically or in any other way.

God created all human beings, and all humanity is created in the image of God. So whenever and wherever Christians see injustice, we have a responsibility to oppose it and work for the liberation of all people so that they can be free to become whom God created them to be and to reach their God- given potential. Whatever "isms" (racism, sexism, ageism, and economic oppression) we may see in our society that are contrary to God's word should be confronted by the church. We must take seriously that portion of the Lord's Prayer when we say "thy will be done on earth as it is in heaven." Part of our calling as Christians in the church is to work to transform this world so that it will be consistent with the will and way of God. That's a hard task to undertake, but God has given us His Spirit to empower us to be able to stand for what is righteous and fair in society.

When we seriously read the bible, we can see clearly that God always has a strong inclination towards those who are oppressed, ostracized, downtrodden, abused, poor, excluded and forgotten by our society. God has called us in the church to be a voice for those who often have no voice for themselves in addition to ministering to their needs in tangible ways. Social justice ministry can change a community, city, state or nation; and will inevitably change the world. As Christians, we are not supposed to be "so heavenly minded that we are no earthly good!" Therefore, just as Jesus was socially conscious in His ministry and transformed people's lives, we should do likewise. Regarding social justice ministry, we should remember the following:

1) The Church is called by God to transform the culture, not be transformed by it.

There is no doubt that the church of today can and should be a very influential participant in shaping society. Because we proclaim God's authority to be superior to politicians, the rich, and other movers and shakers in the country; the church is often viewed and treated as if it is simply another organization that must be managed and controlled by various power structures in society. But the church must always remember that although our ministry and activity may have political implications, our agenda is primarily spiritual and theological. When we carry out God's calling in our lives in its' totality we are transforming the world in a way that makes it consistent with the Kingdom of God on earth. We are always mindful that God has called us to transform the world, not conform to it. So, our ministry is always seeking ways to make God's will a reality on earth.

2) The Gospel of Jesus Christ is relevant in addressing all the "isms".

The Gospel of Jesus Christ does not discriminate the same way that human beings tend to in society. Jesus openly and lovingly invites "whosoever" will come to Him and believe in Him to enter a relationship with Him. In that way, the Gospel is liberating for people in the world. Wherever people are being oppressed by racism, ageism, sexism, or any other "isms"; the Gospel message proclaims that God loves the whole world despite any and all human differences.

3) Social justice ministry seeks to help those who are victims and may have no voice.

This ministry is important because there are so many people who don't have the ability to have their cries heard by the oppressors who are being unjust and unfair. In some cases, the oppressors hear the cries of the people, but they just don't care. Social justice ministry holds oppressors accountable in our society, and makes them listen to the voice of the oppressed. Individuals may not be heard or regarded, but when the church of Jesus Christ organizes itself to speak on an issue; the powers that be must pay attention. So, when the church demands change in society, the collective voice is heard loud and clear!

Application for the Reader: Reflections on Chapters 11 and 12

Here, we have been told what we might feel is the obvious –

to go forth and spread the Word of God – to talk about your love of Jesus Christ. We have also been challenged to stand up for what is right when we see racist or other unkind behavior. And, true, we do know all this; we know what we should do. Do we, however, always stand up and do what we should do? We know what is right; do we make that known to others?

Conclusions for the Reader:
What else do you believe now?

Whether we are new to the church or were born and raised in it, it is important to know what we believe doctrinally and why we believe it. Christians who have seriously embraced their faith as a way of life and not just a once-a-week habit would want to have at least a basic knowledge of their own doctrinal beliefs as well as an ability to articulate them in the course of normal everyday conversation.

> **Whether we are new to the church or were born and raised in it, it is important to know what we believe doctrinally and why we believe it.**

This issue lies at the heart of what it means to be a disciple of Jesus Christ. If we are going to be followers and learners of Jesus Christ, then we must understand what that means and what the implications of that confession are for how we live our lives every day.

This issue is also at the heart of evangelism. We cannot share the Good News of the Gospel of Jesus Christ with others effectively if we don't understand what its' meaning and substance is on some basic level. In these days and times, evangelism must be about more than just initially sharing personal testimonies and experiences about God with others; it must also include some basic understanding of the substance of the beliefs that we accept and embrace by faith along with the practice of living a life that is shaped and formed by them.

If we are going to be followers and learners of Jesus Christ, then we must understand what that means and what the implications of that confession are for how we live our lives every day.

Every individual Christian and every church must take this calling and challenge seriously. When we *don't* know what we believe and why, it will affect how we view ourselves, how we view others inside and outside of the church, and even how we view God and God's church. When we *don't* know what we believe, it will affect how we treat one another within the church, the community and the world. It affects what type of hierarchies of power that we construct in the church and the community, and it will affect how we vote in elections. Not knowing what we believe will affect the kinds of decisions we make in the church as well as the kinds of issues that we prioritize in the life of the church.

Indeed, when we *don't* know what we believe and why; we then become church people who are most vulnerable to becoming conformed to this world culture rather than being transformed into the radical counter-cultural disciples of Jesus Christ that God has called us to be. This transformation that God desires for every Christian necessitates a renewal of the mind with new knowledge and understanding of who God is, how God works in human history, and what God has revealed and is revealing to us in Jesus Christ, the Bible and in daily life.

When we in the church understand with greater clarity what we believe and why; our personal lives, families, churches, and communities will be greatly improved and enhanced because we will better understand what it means to be faithful to God and how to truly let the image of God within each of us shine forth in the midst of this world.

About the Author

Reverend Dr. Jesse T. Williams, Jr. serves as the Senior Pastor of Convent Avenue Baptist Church in Harlem, New York. He leads the 3000 member congregation in a dynamic, ministry- focused, socially-conscious ministry which operates based on the tenets of Worship, Discipleship, Stewardship, Fellowship and Leadership; and is a spiritual and social landmark church in the community of Harlem and the city of New York. His spiritually-anointed preaching ministry blesses thousands across the tri-state area and throughout the country via television, radio and live internet broadcasts on a weekly basis.

He has 21 years of pastoral ministry experience, 28 years as a licensed preacher of the Gospel, and has also previously served on the faculty of Eden Theological Seminary in St. Louis, Missouri as Professor of Congregational Studies for 7 years.

He holds a Bachelor's Degree in Mechanical Engineering and a Bachelor's Degree in Business Administration, both from the University of Kansas. He also holds both the Master of Divinity Degree and the Doctor of Ministry Degree from Eden Theological Seminary.

He is married to Gelaine R. Williams and they are the blessed and proud parents of one son; Jesse III.

Need additional copies?

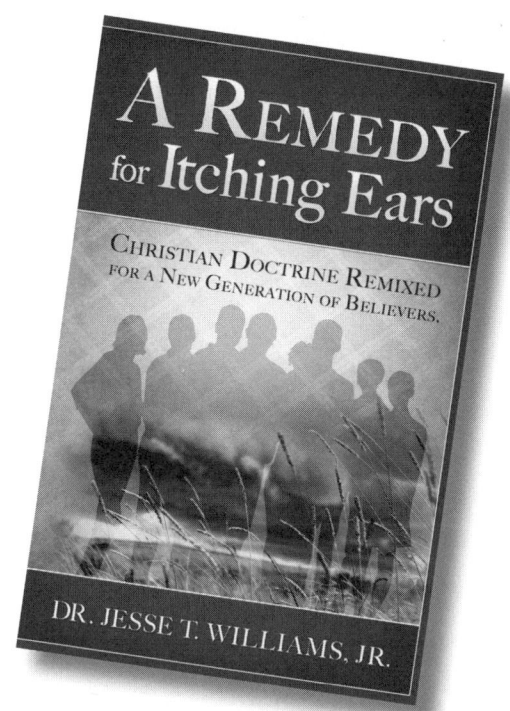

To order more copies of

A REMEDY for Itching Ears,

contact **jtwilliams@conventchurch.org** or

visit **www.remedyforitchingears.com** or

NewBookPublishing.com

- ❐ Order online at:
  NewBookPublishing.com/Bookstore

- ❐ Call 877-311-5100 or

- ❐ Email Info@NewBookPublishing.com

Call for multiple copy discounts!

Reliance Media